Tumultuous
The Apogee

Y.R. PERRY

Copyright © 2021 by Y.R. Perry

All rights reserved. This book or any portion thereof may not be reproduced or used in any manner whatsoever without the express written permission of the publisher except for the use of brief quotations in a book review.

Printed in the United States of America

ISBN: 978-0-578-90106-0

First Printing, 2021

For information, write:

yperry92@gmail.com

Dedication

Worth lies in what you value.
My prayer is that you always value self first, above all things.
Something of value that has been broken, can still hold the same value when the pieces are put back together.
They will be as if brand new with just the right glue.
Put the pieces of your life together with much faith, prayer, and God, that's the best glue.
Crown On Ladies!

Tumultuous The Apogee

If you have read *Tumultuous* and *Tumultuous Too,* your mind is probably reeling from the turn of events from one book to the next. I wrote those two books in character form to excite and intrigue, but to also bring to the forefront, real life situations that happened in my life and in the life of some of my closest friends. I was afraid of being emotionally transparent or mentally naked. That's the route I chose and it has healed me of my past in many ways. To empty out my soul onto paper freed me and healed me of my insanity.

Now, I will speak freely and you will read it directly from me. My prayer is that you find solace in what you might be today, and the story does the same for you. If not, write your own novel and even if you never publish it, find the freedom of purging yourself on paper. Now, I'm emptied out to start anew. I'm no psychiatrist by any means. I'm only a woman with experience and wisdom that I've learned from.

Chapter after chapter, I will give you my personal advice and perspective on life's journeys and how I saved my soul in the process.

Acknowledgments

Editor: Marvin D. Cloud

Cover Design: Keith Crear of Grizzly Media

Back photo cred: Touche' Harvey of Touche' Studios

Table of Contents

Introduction		1
Chapter 1	Getting out of her Shoes	3
Chapter 2	Empty Darkness	9
Chapter 3	Divorcing Sex	13
Chapter 4	What's My Purpose Now?	19
Chapter 5	Her Shoes Hurt, Too	25
Chapter 6	Forced to Fly	31
Chapter 7	Jaws of a Dog	37
Chapter 8	What Could Have Killed Me...	47
Chapter 9	Stop Letting Him Breadcrumb You, Sis	55
Chapter 10	Being an Energy Outlet	61
Chapter 11	Eyes Forward	67
Chapter 12	Friend or F.O.E. (Friend of Opportunity Expert)	71

Chapter 13	Artichoke or Onion	75
Chapter 14	Why be Beautiful?	81
Chapter 15	Loud Silence	87
Chapter 16	Seeking Approval From the Underqualified	93
Chapter 17	The Time I Decided to Live and not Die	97
Chapter 18	Mr. Handsome, Well-To-Do, And Six Foot Two?	103
Chapter 19	Quietly Making Noise	109
Chapter 20	Hey, Dark and Lovely	113
Chapter 21	Unpacking Pain	119
Chapter 22	Am I Good Enough?	125
Chapter 23	I Surrender	131
Chapter 24	The Coming of Me	137
Chapter 25	The Straw That Could Have Broke Me Built Me	141

INTRODUCTION: TUMULTUOUS "THE APOGEE"

Well, you know I couldn't resist the urge to tell you the end of my story, (in my Betty Wright voice) Lol. If you want to know if there was life after all the pain of *Tumultuous* and *Tumultuous Too*, let me tell you this, there is.

Was it easy? Absolutely not, but in *Tumultuous Apogee*, I will speak to you directly; no hiding behind characters. Only my truth of how I maintained my mind absent from things that would destroy me again, and retained self-love and confidence.

Many of my *Tumultuous* readers want to know who Yvette fell into the arms of after her short time in jail? Who was the man that came to her rescue? Where did it all go from there?

The answers to your questions lay at the end of this book. They are all things of the past and lessons learned; mistakes made never to be repeated. Now, let's dive into *Tumultuous the Apogee*! I will walk you through how I got over obstacle after obstacle in an effort to remain standing, stay alive physically, and not die mentally. Also I will share nuggets of inspiration and advice that I hope will help you discover the "you within you" that should always come first.

CHAPTER 1
GETTING OUT OF HER SHOES

One of the most valuable things my mom ever told me was for me to be better than her and to never walk in her shoes. Growing up as a young woman I didn't understand what that meant. My mom was beautiful. She had beautiful hair, a nice figure, and flawless skin to die for. All of the hottest clothes and shoes hung in her closet. Oftentimes, my sisters, cousins, and I, would play dress up in her heels and clothing when she was at work. My mom threw the best parties in the projects. There would be cars lined up for what seemed like miles, and our apartment would be packed with people; family, friends, and friends of friends. My sisters and I, and sometimes our cousins, if they spent the night, would peek out of the door and watch everyone dance and drink. We hoped we did not get caught because we were supposed to be asleep. My mom had it going on. She had beauty, popularity, and the love of the neighborhood. Why wouldn't I want to be like her?

Did I mention she had amazing clothes and shoes? As I continued to grow up into a young lady, I would learn why she said never walk in her shoes, and why it was the most valuable advice she could have ever told me. I watched her go through mental and physical abuse from a man she loved as I felt helpless, because there was nothing I could do. Coupled with a short battle with drug addiction, foster care became a part of my life. In return, I became a runaway at the age of 16. You see, to me, as long as I was under the same roof, I had no choice but to walk in her shoes. Being a teenager in school I tried to belong, only to arrive at home after school some days and not know what the climate of my dwelling would be like. Examples I saw at home were mostly all I knew, and what I saw on TV. As I grew up, I mimicked her to a degree, along with some of what I saw on TV. Drug use never played a part in my life, but I accepted a little abuse and stayed a little longer than I should have. Now when I say, "a little," I mean just that because one thing I did do was fight back. When I would ask my mom why she never fought back, she would reply, "it only makes it worse." Nevertheless, I fought back anyway and I left. She never did.

Who would have known that as I grew up and became a wife and mother, I would still sometimes walk down an emotional path, relationship-wise that my mom would repeatedly travel. When life got tough, I would often hear her in the back of my mind say, *get out of my shoes*. When I would call her and tell her what I was going through, those would be the exact words she would say to me. Somehow, at some point, I still remained in those shoes. In spite of all the great advice she gave me, my question to her was always, "why?" Why did she stay? I honestly believe her choices to stay and not leave still plagues her today. Unsatisfied with the way life has turned out, never married but always having the desire to be a wife, she's still mentally stuck in that world, as she accepts more than she should allow in her life. If only she knew the value she would possess if she only chose to be happy and get out of those shoes.

To be happy is a choice we all have the option to make. Before I became stuck in a world where I could not see my way out of, I chose happiness. Getting into that place was definitely not easy. You see, after you have dwelt in darkness for a long time, bright lights will hurt your eyes and you have to wait for your vision to focus in order to see clearer. It's called darkness adaptation. When in darkness, the eyes become sensitive and can increase sensitivity over a period of time. This is called rhodopsin. Regeneration is a process and permanent blindness is rumored to occur if left in the dark for too long. This is much like life situations that may occur. If you decide to dwell in darkness longer than necessary, you will run the risk of possibly becoming permanently blind. You become blind to your own faults, blind to your true enemies, blind to love, real friends and the true meaning of family. Most importantly, you don't hear God's yielding voice that tries to gently nudge and steer you in better directions.

I made a conscious decision not to dwell in darkness. Although when I came out of it, the adjustment period was painful, in the sense of learning new ways and adapting new habits. I continued to seek the light and the more I did, my vision corrected itself and I saw clearer. All that being said, sometimes darkness can become a comfortable place to be. Know that coming out of darkness takes work, or it may hurt, therefore you choose the latter, and stay there because it's comfortable. My advice to you is don't risk complete blindness. Fight for the light. Adjust your vision and set yourself free. The comfort of peace awaits you.

Learn from past transgressions, pave your own way. Your destiny awaits you!

Y. R. Perry

CHAPTER 2

EMPTY DARKNESS

Have you ever been in complete darkness? Perhaps not mentally, but physically? Before the lights were turned off, you could see where everything was, but once the lights turned off, those things seem to have disappeared leaving nothing but a dark space. Although nothing had moved, you still found yourself stumbling around to find items, reaching out with your hands to find where you knew them to be. Maybe you bumped into a few things and stubbed your toe on the corner of a bed. That is painful I might add!

I know I'm not the only one who has awakened in the middle of the night to use the bathroom and in an effort not to completely wake up, I refused to turn on the light. I'd run into things while going in the wrong direction. I reached out my hands into the darkness in an effort to find my way, when all I had to do was turn on the light. My pathway would be illuminated which would have made it easy for me to see what's in front of me. There would have been no need to have gone in the wrong direction, bump into walls, and hurt myself. In life, sometimes we make decisions not to turn on mental lights. We sometimes figure, "Oh, I got this!"

When darkness comes, sometimes the mind becomes a little confused. Just know that all is still in the same place. Whether the lights are on or off it, doesn't change with the flip of a switch, you have to physically move them in order for the change to take place. When you walk in the dark, the mind still sends you off course and causes you to be a little unsure of the location of the clear path.

Today, choose to stop stumbling around in darkness, although it can be a little discomforting to be completely awakened; mind, body, and spirit. Life is much better when you choose to see a clearer picture of what lies ahead. No more bumping into walls and hurting yourself on the sharp corners of life. You hold the key. It's all in your hands and it is as simple as choosing to flip the switch and make the change. Moving in darkness can be a slow and unsure process. Even with your eyes wide open in darkness, your vision sees emptiness and confusion. There may be some valuable things left in the darkness but with the lights on, you get to choose what you take forward with you and what you should leave behind. Turn on your light today.

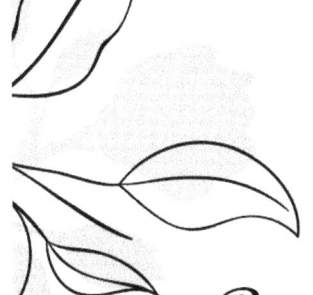

Become your own beacon of light so you may oneday direct someone out of darkness...

Y.R. Perry

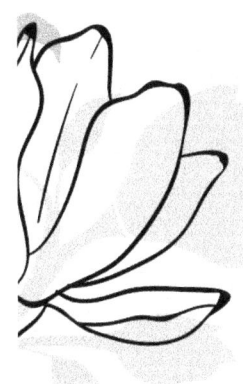

CHAPTER 3

DIVORCING SEX

Being a woman who was into sexual intimacy with the person I was involved with or felt deeply for, I began to use it as a coping mechanism or a means of resolving issues. As I began to mature, I discovered it was only a temporary band-aid. Once that euphoric feeling disappeared, the problems were still there. Women, and some men, often make the mistake of intimately giving too much of themselves while we try to hold on to something that will never change. No matter how much of a bedroom acrobat you may be, it will not make anyone change a person who chooses to be unfaithful to you. To be unfaithful is definitely a choice, not a mistake.

To be faithful is a decision made by someone because they deeply care about you as a person, and your feelings, and they value your feelings towards them. Some of the most beautiful and successful women in the world have experienced this on several different levels, and still live this way at this moment. I was once *her* in my marriage. When I was married, I considered my now ex-husband a triple threat.

Let me put you in my business a little bit and go on to say, his fellatio game was amazing, and God blessed him abundantly with endowment and the gift of the desire to please a woman to no end. Not only did he have that, he was monetarily sound and materialistically gave me anything I wanted. Sounds like every woman's fantasy or dream, right? Soon after all the euphoria of sexual haze wore off, and materialistic things started to get old, the one thing I desired was, fidelity, something he chose, not to give me. I received phone calls from other women and found him chatting on the phone with them when he thought I was asleep. He constantly made sure he had his phone with him at all times, even if it was just a trip to the bathroom. I was no dummy though; I knew exactly what was going on. Yet, I was still willing to do whatever it took to keep my marriage. I changed my hair, lost weight when he said I looked a little thick, and gained weight when he said I looked a little too thin. I gave him attention as often as he needed to make him happy, even on days when I felt totally and mentally drained. I hoped I could be everything he needed. It wasn't enough. He still cheated and he still lied.

Often, as a cover-up, he would buy me expensive gifts. Over time I began to realize material things didn't matter. I desired more. My marriage was falling apart, and my husband was a serial cheater. After several years, I mustered up the energy and strength to finally leave the marriage because I felt like I deserved more, only to find myself repeating the same pattern in relationships as a single woman. I held on to a bunch of nothing, for nothing. Yet I continued to hold on, pulled out all the sexual tricks that I thought would keep the relationship solid. It was not the glue I needed at all. I quickly and painfully learned that having a vagina does not help keep a man who does not want to be kept, no matter how great he says it is. If he's the unfaithful type or the never satisfied type, he will constantly look for the challenge of finding and experiencing better. So-called relationships became more like recreational activities. You play for a little while and when it doesn't keep your interest, you're off to the next activity. You find yourself giving it your all, having no idea that you were the only one interested in playing to win, or had hopes of winning in spite of what was blatantly obvious.

After my divorce and a few losses in the world of dating, I decided to take a break. I realized I needed to heal myself in an effort to be a better me and in order to make better choices. The unwillingness from my husband to be faithful, and me being in relationships shortly thereafter, where I gave of myself with no commitment or direction, began to take a mental toll on me. I second-guessed my worth, my looks, my skin tone, and my level of success. It got to the point I fell into a deep depression, but no one knew it. I carried it and wore it well. You would never see it on my face or be able to tell from my social media posts. I kept smiling. I put on makeup and did my hair while I cried on the inside, wondering *what I was doing wrong?* One of the tell-tell signs of a woman who is going through something, is a change in her appearance. One of the things my grandmother instilled in me was, "Never look like what you're going through."

So I made up in my mind to separate myself from the one thing that men love and I loved as much, SEX. Sex can definitely cloud your judgment and make you stay in situations longer than you need to. It can also make you feel loved when love can be the furthest thing from the truth. Sex can make you believe if you do it right, you can own someone. In some cases, that can be true depending on that person's mindset. For me, I always associated sex with love and falling in love. No matter how I tried to mentally prepare myself to be the hit it and quit it woman, it was not in my

DNA. Over time, it seems as if the world made this drastic change to where no one had sex to fall in love anymore, or to ultimately end up in a committed monogamous relationship. I decided to divorce sex for a while. Now when I say divorce sex, I went into a period of celibacy. To this day, I can say it was the best decision I could have ever made for myself.

In a world where the term "side piece" is worn like a badge of honor and more men than I would have imagined come out of the closet, this was best for me. Divorcing sex, or making a conscious decision to become celibate for a while, allowed me to think clearer, work on my self-worth, value the things I could offer a man, and demand that he values me. I took the keys back and built a new house within myself. One of self-love, value, confidence, and determination. These are the keys that I will not relinquish to anyone who is not willing to love me as I deserve, build with me, within me and grow with me. Also I see the greater good in me that will serve us both. Take your keys back and hold on to them. Only give them to the person who will open you up to everything your heart desires and more!

Learn to develop feelings above the belt first! Often what's below will fail you at first...

Y.R. Perry

CHAPTER 4
WHAT'S MY PURPOSE NOW?

Now that I wasn't willing to participate in the one thing I felt would draw me closer to a man, or cause him to possibly fall in love when he failed to see my other existing attributes, I didn't know where to begin. Nevertheless, it was time to find my purpose. Some women feel our purpose is to marry, please our husbands, cook, have and raise children. We think that makes our lives complete. That may be a true perception for some women, and if that's what you desire and it completes you, I applaud you. I'm all for it. What happens though, when you find yourself 40-ish, married before, now divorced, with children who are now grown, and you are a single empty nester with a few unsuccessful tries at relationships? You have a nice car, a place of your own, and you work every day at a job that affords you the lifestyle you desire. That should be great, right? For some it is.

One might say, "It's the best type of life. You should be living it up, girl!" What do you do when you have done that and years have gone by. In my case, it was 10 years and counting and it started to pale in comparison to what I had imagined my life to be once my children were grown up. Some may enjoy that life until the day of their demise. Others such as myself, desire companionship and oneness with another human being. In an effort not to make the same mistake as before, I had to find a new purpose now that I was minus the husband and small children. No one could give me that. It was something I had to figure out all on my own.

First, I knew I had to continue to heal myself mentally, because being an emotionally shattered person, sometimes will blind you from your purpose. My steps to healing began with purging myself of harmful emotions which brought about my decision to become an author. At first, it started out as journaling, and then after much coercion, I decided to write a book. In my writing, I was transparent in an indirect way. The way I chose to do so was more entertaining and brought about a sense of relatable realness. It's almost like knowing a friend's breath stinks and you want to tell them but you can't gather the nerve to say it directly. You might offer them a mint or a piece of gum in hopes that they would catch on because you don't know how they would handle you being so direct. Whether directly or indirectly, I was able to purge my shortcomings and some of my experiences with friends and start my healing process through my writing.

A lot of times as human beings, we don't realize how much of other people's energy we store on top of our own, by listening to their stories and tying into their emotions. This is especially true if that person is near and dear to us. Realistically, I purged myself of negative energy that was brought on by my choices along with others I stored on top. Once I emptied the vast majority, I didn't have to look for my purpose. Purpose found me. How can you see your purpose if the things you're consumed with weigh you down or fill you up to where you can't fathom the idea of having purpose. Purge yourself and make room for your purpose. However you see fit to do so, join a dance group, become a part of your local actors community, join your church choir or join a gym. Exercise releases positive endorphins. Meditate and dedicate 10 minutes to clear your head of all the mind chatter. Find a quiet space free of noise, distractions, and increase your meditation time as you go. You can do as I did, write it out. Whether you publish it or not, you have emptied your storage and prepared a place for your new purpose.

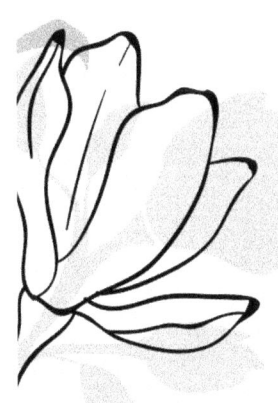

There's purpose in everything YOU do and everything that happens to YOU. Build on your Purpose....

Y.R. Perry

CHAPTER 5
HER SHOES HURT, TOO

Have you ever been in a setting where there are designer shoes everywhere or had a friend or someone you admired from a distance who always dressed nice, and wore the bad ass clothing? You dress pretty nice as well, you went out, did your hair, nails, and make-up and looked just as flawless as her. The only thing she had on you was her Christian Louboutins or Manolo Blahniks versus your Steve Madden heels or the shoes from JustFab that you thought were amazing.

One evening, while attending an event, I happened to run into a woman like that. While I fixed my hair and re-applied my lipstick in the mirror, she entered the restroom with her two friends and she gripped her foot pain. She was wearing a pair of Christian Louboutins.

Pulling them off for a second to relieve her feet, she said, "As much as I pay for these shoes, they shouldn't hurt this bad!"

Meanwhile I comfortably stood there in my $19.99 specials from JustFab that I bought online, but I was slightly envious and I wished I had a pair of those shoes with the red soles. For some reason, those shoes meant in my mind that you had status. It meant you had arrived and you could walk among the elite. That's what I thought at that time. I also remember her stating that she had only been at the party for two hours and that she would have to get really tipsy to not feel her feet for the duration of the party.

As for me, I had not been at the party the same amount of time, but I was dressed equally as nice. The only difference was those shoes. The shoes range anywhere from $500.00 up into the thousands. I had one drink but she needed more to numb her pain. After a few more minutes she shoved the shoes back on her feet and proceeded to make her way back to the dance floor. Putting on a smile she walked out as if her feet never hurt.

Over time, I would see this woman out and about on a regular basis and in different elements. She always wore a big smile and shoes that she always looked great, but were probably killing her feet. Ultimately, I got to know her and found that she dealt with far more pain than her feet. Behind her smile, she dealt with an adulterous husband. They put on airs if they were the perfect couple, but at home behind closed doors, she wanted something one would think is far less expensive than the shoes she wore in pain on a regular basis. It seemed too much to ask of her husband, but she wanted his loyalty and commitment to her and only her. She wanted him to adhere to the vows they took before family and friends and God, to keep thee only unto her, until death do them part.

I've been down that road before. I have put on airs in front of friends and family and was showered with expensive guilt gifts by my husband as if that would make up for his transgressions. At first I loved it; brand names purses, shoes, and diamonds, you name it. Who wouldn't? There also comes a time though, when it gets old. I wanted more. I wanted what was promised to me and what I deserved as a wife, a faithful and loyal husband. I deserved it! Needless to say, I never got it. I married him twice in hopes that it would be better and it was the same as before the second time around.

As the old saying goes, "a leopard never changes its stripes." Although there are some men who do change, he has to make that change. There's nothing a woman can do to force that change. He must desire to see you happy and not hurt. Then and only then, will a change come about. Never envy what another woman has, because sometimes behind her smile and designer shoes, she carries pain that some can't begin to fathom. Never wish for or envy what you see on the exterior because the interior holds things you probably couldn't handle.

By the way, I finally got a pair of those Christian Louboutins and they do hurt like hell and cost a lot! Often, I alternate them with my JustFab shoes because I love shoes regardless of cost. My JustFab shoes get more wear than my Christian Louboutins because I rather be comfortable than put on airs and be in pain for the masses. Always be in position to shift out of pain when necessary. Don't stay stuck in it because it looks good and it's the hottest thing going. Find a way to shift out of pain, in a less costly way and continue to look good while doing so. If it costs you your happiness and your most valuable asset, your soul, it's not worth it.

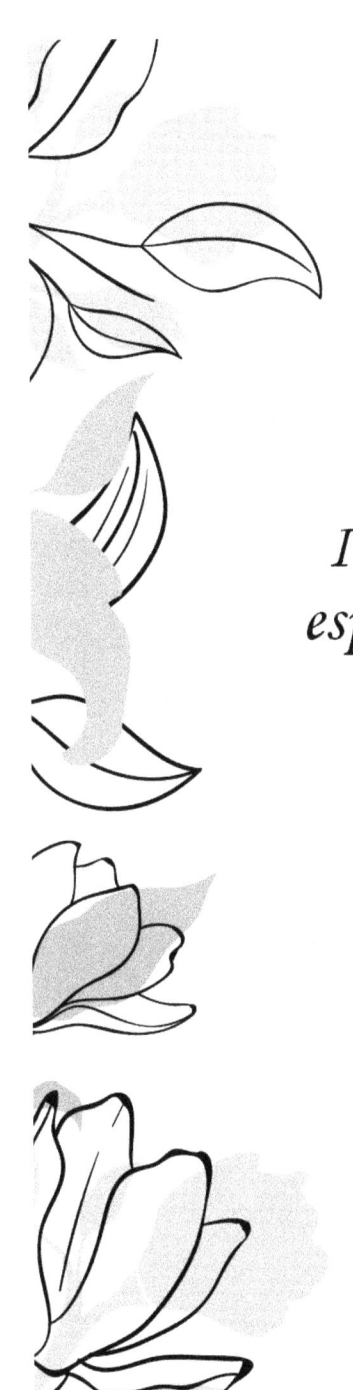

*Walk your own walk...
It was designed
especially for you!*

Y. R. Perry

CHAPTER 6
FORCED TO FLY

Situations may come about in your life where you have no choice but to move forward. No matter what, you have to press on. Sure, you can choose not to get out of bed sometimes because you're having a bad day. You can keep your blinds closed and not want to move, including not even take a shower. Coming from a family that battled mental health issues on one side coupled with depression and anxiety issues, I saw and experienced a lot.

Determined not to succumb to what ultimately would catch up with me in the future, I fought hard. Eventually, it caught up with me. I had a bad case of anxiety and an on and off battle with depression that I learned to hide well from the world, my children, family, and friends. I didn't know what it was until I got a little older. Being divorced twice and being a single mother didn't make it any easier. I had a choice to make and that choice became clear each time I looked at the two beings I brought into the world. They deserved the best of me. There was no time to do less than that.

When my son was about 15 or 16 years old, we were in the kitchen and we casually talked about life. I can't quite remember how we got on the subject of death, but my son looked at me with tears in his eyes and said, "Mom I don't know what I would do without you or if something happened to you." He then became extremely sad at that moment. I put my hand underneath his chin and lifted his head so that he could look me in my eyes.

I told him, "You know what I would want you to do? I would want you to be the best man you could be." Then I gave him a big lingering hug and told him, "Don't worry, I'll be here for a while."

He wasn't the wiser concerning the mental demons I fought often in order for me to be the best possible mother I could be to him and his sister. Later, I discovered that the anxiety and depression I experienced would trickle down to my daughter.

My daughter would say, "Mom, I think I need to talk to someone. I'm feeling depressed and I don't know why."

I never questioned her confession, because I already saw it, even though I had asked her about it before and she denied it. I was glad she finally came to me. Then, I begin to blame and question myself. What did I do wrong? Was I not there enough? What can I do for her not to be depressed and experience those feelings I've endured? I did my best. I kept her from encountering any of the hands I was dealt in my childhood. Why did it happen? I wanted her to snap out of it, but it doesn't work like that. All I could do was be there. I had a daughter who although fully grown, still needed me and a son who couldn't bear the thought of ever losing me. That meant no matter what, I needed to pull myself together. I had to beat this. I could not let it destroy me to the point I wasn't there for them.

There was no way I could just say to them, "You're grown now. Go on and live your life, and I will go live mine." That was not an option.

I moved forward from that moment. Every time I felt like giving up or not getting up, I thought about them living a life without me under those circumstances. After all, we were all we had. The Three Musketeers is what we called ourselves. Even in my darkest hours, when I felt like I couldn't go on, I would think of them. After all, your children are mostly a product of you, the experience you give them, the things you say to them, and most definitely what you show them.

My children, although young adults at the time still needed me to fuel them. In hindsight, they also fueled me. I had no choice but to continue flying. The days when anxiety and depression got me down would be sometimes extremely difficult to desire to move, but I would not stay down. I only had to think about them. I thought of more ways to win and make our lives and futures easier. It may be difficult sometimes and you might not see a way out, find yourself a strong reason why and force yourself to fly! Someone or something needs you to carry on. There are skies untouched, limits not broken, and words that can only come from your lips, not spoken. Words can empower or fuel someone and maybe in return, the fuel that you give them will be returned to you one day. Force yourself to fly!

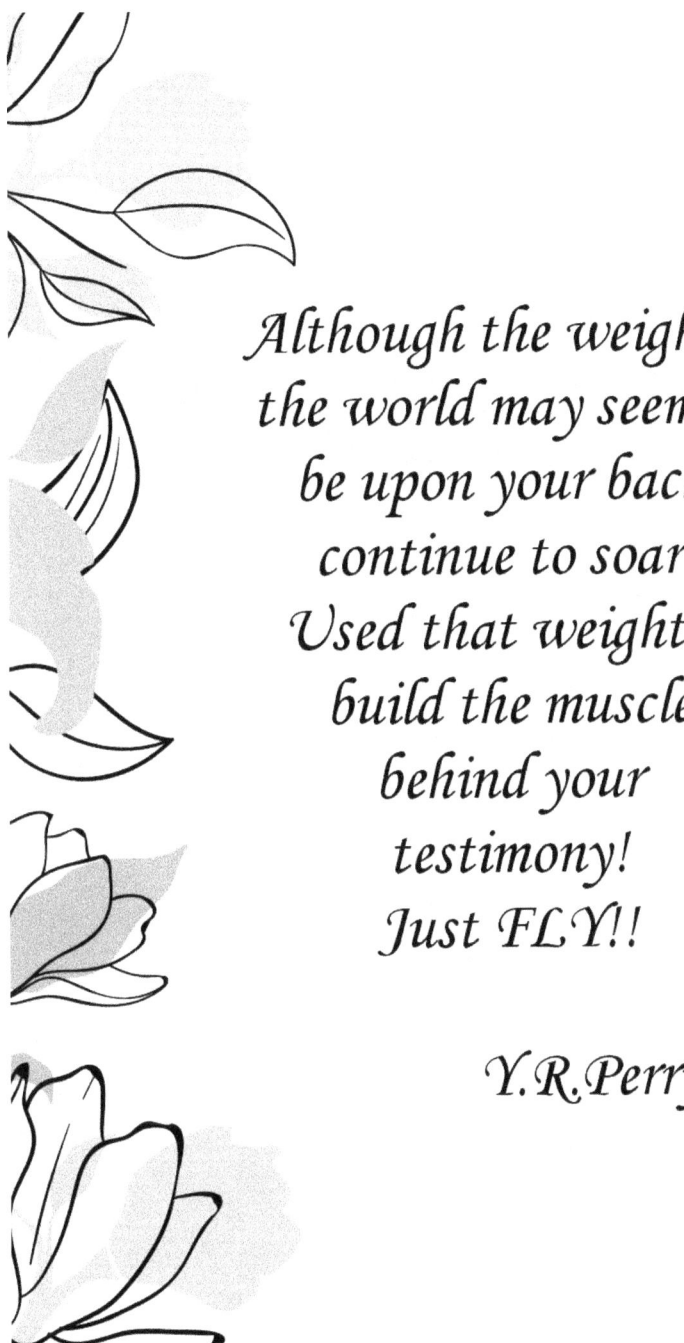

Although the weight of the world may seem to be upon your back, continue to soar! Used that weight to build the muscle behind your testimony! Just FLY!!

Y.R.Perry

CHAPTER 7

JAWS OF A DOG

This chapter by far was the toughest chapter for me to write, but here it goes. This occurred at a time in my life when I felt I had completely purged myself of hurt, pain, and trauma. It was a night with someone I trusted who threatened to send me back into a dark place I fought so hard to get out of. I ran into an old friend who proved to be a person I should have left in my past. Have you ever spent time with someone and for some reason, things never progressed beyond friendship? Finding myself getting back reacquainted with a gentleman I met some years ago after he was released from the federal pen would beg the term "let sleeping dogs lie."

Initially, when I found out this tidbit of information, I was turned off but ultimately I listened to his story and learn why he was incarcerated. His story was that he was incarcerated due to drug distribution. *Okay, not bad* I thought. It wasn't due to raping or killing anyone, right? He now walked the straight and narrow. He had his own place and thrived after his stint in prison. Everyone deserves a second chance, right? We went out on a few dates, but I couldn't get the thought out of my head that he had been incarcerated. Many questions ran through my mind. I had never dated someone who had been in prison before as far as I knew. My apprehensions soon led me to distance myself. He was tall, muscular, and good-looking with an amazing smile. I still couldn't shake the thought no matter what. When I met him, he seemed to be getting his life back on track, but after many relationships where I was that woman who stuck by her man's side until he got on his feet, this time I wasn't willing to do it. Over the years, we touched base with one another, on and off, here and there, and then we lost touch again. A few years went by, and he reached out to me via social media. He mentioned he was married but was going through a divorce and wanted to know if we could meet up? We did and at this time he was extremely established, more than before. He lived in his own place, owned a couple of cars, and had been on his job for some time now and looked even better than ever.

Normally, I wouldn't date a guy who was separated, because to me, you're still married until the papers are signed. Nevertheless, that smile, that body, and that charm made me forego my thoughts of being morally correct. Besides, I knew him before he was married. That was the way I reasoned with myself for going against the grain of what I deemed to be proper. Probably out of loneliness, I had to convince myself and I thought, *maybe it was meant to be*. You know, us reconnecting after all this time. Thereafter we talked on the phone for hours and reminisced about how he boldly stepped to me in a club full of guys after being released for two years and how when he first met me, he barely had anything, but look at him now. I congratulated him on his success and being off papers. I also expressed sympathy over the demise of his marriage. He seemed to be still in mourning over his marriage but he insisted it was for the best. Of course, when questioned, everything was blamed on the wife. The only one thing he owned up to was slapping her out of anger because of a remark she made that challenged his manhood.

Expressing deep remorse, he said it was the first time and last time. Although there's no reason to hit a woman, I could see how the statement he said she made could possibly set a man off. I was a listening ear and in some instances I felt sorry for him. Needless to say, I dated him in spite of my thoughts of never dating a man before he was completely divorced. I began a courtship where there was friendship, so to speak. The courtship consisted of going out to dinner, perhaps meeting up after work, doing dinner at my place or his place, and overnight stays without any sexual encounters. I had expressed that I was celibate and I hoped my next sexual encounter would be my last and ultimately lead to marriage. Prayerfully, it would be with a man I loved and who loved me.

He said he understood and that it was not a big deal to him. He was content with our friendship and comfortable with it while he went through the divorce. As I drove home from work each day, I always had to pass the exit off the freeway that led to his home. He would ask me to stop and give him a hug. I said I would. I knew how hard and lonely a divorce can be. Been there and done that.

As time went on, he encouraged me to bring clothes and spend the night to shave 30 minutes off my commute to work. I enjoyed his company. He had a nice apartment and it was neatly furnished and clean for a man. I had been spending a lot of time with him anyways, so why not?

Periodically, I began to do just that. We would not be intimate and he seemed to be cool with it. I told him once his divorce papers were signed, I would be open to changing the course of my celibacy journey for him. Our time spent together grew as well as my feelings for him. But I still stood my ground concerning my celibacy journey. His court date to sign paperwork and finalize his divorce was a couple of days away. The day finally came and I was there to support him. The next night after everything was finalized, I was at home getting ready for bed. I received a call from him. He said he needed some company because he was having a hard time adjusting to the end of his marriage although he knew it was for the best. Me being me, and having been there before, I saw it as an opportunity to comfort a friend and possible future mate. Also, he lived 30 minutes closer to my job.

I responded, "Okay." I packed some items and was on my way. We hung out that night, played cards, watched movies, had pizza and a few drinks. He had been drinking before I got there. We really enjoyed each other's company. It seemed to keep his mind off things. Then, we eventually fell asleep. Right before daybreak, I was startled out of my sleep. I was being aggressively pinned down with a six foot three, 220 lb., muscular body on top of me. Using one of his hands to wrestle my hands above my head and pin them down, and the other to reach inside the leg opening of the shorts I wore that night and rip away at my panties. In a state of shock, and half asleep, I was disoriented. It was dark and I could feel the weight of this man's body on top of me. He ripped away at my clothing and growled like he was a dog.

I gained my composure and began to fight. I knew that if I could just get my knees up and in between myself and him, I could get him off me. My legs have always been the strongest part of my body. After multiple attempts and struggling I managed to do that. I turned on my side to get out of the bed, and that's when he grabbed me around my waist and pulled me back. He continued to growl like a dog he then flipped me over, held my hands down again and used his face and mouth to go under my shirt and put the other hand into my shorts and pulled at my panties. He then tried to insert himself inside of me. I grew weary of fighting this man who was obviously much stronger than me. I felt like giving up. I started to lose my will to fight. I was tired. I told myself, *if I let him have what he wants, then this would be over.*

Many things ran through my mind. I was like all of the women who may have been at this point in their life, and were afraid and just gave in. However, I refused to let someone take something away from me I wasn't willing to give them. I began to fight! I fought for myself and the women who gave in and were afraid to fight. I got my knees up once more and was able to kick him off me again. The kick was forceful enough that it flipped him onto the other side of the bed. This man pounded his fist on his legs in anger and defeat while still growling! Knowing that he kept a gun under his pillow, I sat up straight with my back against the headboard with my knees pulled up to my chest. I stayed still but ready to fight. He then turned, laid down, and went to sleep. I sat there for a minute scared to move. I heard him snore and I quickly gathered my things as quietly as I could. I began to slide on my shoes but before I could completely get them on, he woke up once again.

I didn't make eye contact with him but I heard him ask, "Are you leaving?"

I responded, "Yes, I'm leaving."

He then said, "You say that like you're never coming back." I was afraid to say the wrong thing at that moment. I didn't want to get attacked again.

I simply stated, "No, I'm not saying that. I got to get to work."

By this time it was getting light outside. I gathered my things and walked towards the door. He walked closely behind me poking me in the back with his erect penis. He taunted me about not looking back at him. All I wanted to do was make it to the door. I thought to myself, *if I could get on the other side of that door, I will be free.* The door opened and I could see daylight on the other side of the door. I power walked and almost ran to my car.

I got to my car and drove away. The farther I got away, the more of the reality of what transpired set in. I cried and shook uncontrollably; the tears filled my eyes to the point where I could hardly see the road ahead. Never in a million years would I have thought I would be in such a position. I blamed myself for what I wore that night, what I smelled like, and for going to his house after I was already ready for bed, even though it was only 9p.m. I blamed myself for casually sleeping in the same bed with him and expecting not to give it up. *It's my fault,* I thought.

I pulled into the far end of the parking lot when I reached work. I sobbed even more. I was confused. What happened? What did I do differently this time? I sat there two hours early for work and tried to gather my composure. I put on makeup to the best of my ability using my car's rear view mirror. I wanted to look as normal as possible at work. Something inside of me had to know why this happened? After multiple times of hanging out with the understanding of where I stood, why?

So I called him and I asked, "Why?"

He answered very cavalierly, "I'm a man. Look, you're good. That was my bad. I'm sorry about that. It will never happen again."

That wasn't good enough for me. That day would in return send me into a state of depression that I would fight for my sanity to climb out of. It could have been the detriment of my soul. At times I had out-of-body moments where I saw myself fighting this man off and the moment I felt like I wanted to give up. I battled with blaming myself for the attack. In an effort to remain sane, I shared it with a few friends. I had to know if I did something wrong? My friends were supportive. One wanted me to contact the authorities, whereas another kind of blamed me for going to his home repeatedly and spending the night without the expectation of sex. Another said it didn't matter; he had no right and if I didn't report it, I should think about the next person he may do this to who won't have the courage to fight. I was stuck and confused and tried to get out of my head. *I wasn't raped*, I told myself to justify not calling the police and filing a report. I didn't want to get caught up in all the litigation and questioning. I chose not to put a black man back in jail. He had gotten out of the system and re-established his life. In that moment, I chose him over myself as I had done in previous relationships. I chose to protect him while I suffered in silence. This incident would plague me while I constantly questioned myself, *Is he doing this to someone else at this moment? Has he done this to someone else in the past?* Maybe it was more to his divorce than what he let on.

I am sharing this story ever so transparently as a cautionary tale, in hopes that it helps someone who feels alone in a situation like this. Never put someone else's well-being before yours. Everyone should be held accountable for their actions. Also try to never put yourself in a position that you are not ready for, no matter if the person tries to make you feel your stance is okay. Choose yourself first. Most definitely, if you ever find yourself caught in the jaws of a dog the way I was, fight! Don't give in. Don't ignore the signs. If for some reason you do find yourself there, know that it's not your fault. You did nothing to warrant that type of behavior. Always listen to your inner voice, and that feeling in your gut. Remember always, "a pair of lips will say anything!"

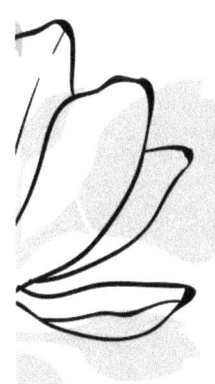

If you make it through one of life's hardest test, be sure to educate the next through your story.....

Y.R. Perry

CHAPTER 8

WHAT COULD HAVE KILLED ME ...

Growing up and becoming a young woman was not what one would consider an easy feat. My grandmother played a major role in my life when it came down to making sure we were well fed and clothed. My grandmother developed glaucoma in her early thirties and for as long as I could remember, she was completely blind, but you would never know it. It never stopped her from doing anything most normal people could do. She cooked, cleaned, washed and folded clothes. My grandmother was a strong woman who didn't depend on anyone for much except driving her around. My grandmother knew her house like the back of her hand. She only depended on our eyes for certain things like telling her what denomination was on a paper bill.

She would get rides from a next door neighbor when we had doctor's appointments or needed to run errands, that is until she bought her own car, then people became her chauffeur. All we had to do was lead her there and she would do all the talking. Everyone knew my grandmother. My mother was young when I was born. As I grew up, my grandmother was a major part of my learning things around the house. Although completely blind, she still taught me how to sew a button onto clothing, how to hem pants, how to open cans with a can opener or without, and how to cook as well. The bulk of me being the woman I am today, came from watching my grandmother beat the odds with no sight. She raised her grandchildren while helping her own children stay on the straight and narrow. The rest came from me being determined not to be the shell of a woman my mom had allowed herself to become at the hands of a man who was 14 years her senior and married. My biggest joy was when I was able to go to my grandma's house and she would teach me something new. I would watch her effortlessly move about her day as she cleaned and cooked.

My cousins and I ran in and out of the house and she would yell, "Close that damn screen door! You're letting all the flies in!"

Those were the good old days. With her, I felt free and happy growing up as a kid. Don't get me wrong, there were some happy times when I lived with my mom, but they were few and far between. Her focus was obscured by a man who claimed to love her, but beat the hell out of her at any given moment. I remember as a child being in my room sleeping and I would hear my mom cry out in pain. That would be the start of a night of hell, because that meant he was beating her yet again. So I would have to lie there with my hands over my ears to muffle the sound until it stopped, or I would have to jump out of the window and go to my grandmother who lived one street over. She was the only one who could make him stop. My mothers cries and pleading didn't stop him, that only seemed to make it worse. My grandmother was the only one he respected, which was funny because he didn't respect my mother.

I would go out of the window in the middle of the night sometimes with my little sister in tow. In her footed pajamas, her little feet made scuffing sounds on the asphalt as we scampered down the street in the middle of the darkness. Once we knocked on the screen door and she was awakened by our little voices, she knew what was going on.

My grandmother grabbed her little 22 that she kept shoved under the mattress, stuck it in her bosom and out into the darkness she went with me holding her hand and leading the way. Sure 'nuff, once my grandmother reached our house, I could hear my mother's cries. My grandmother would yell out his entire government name and say, "you stop it right now, and I mean right now!" And he would stop. Then he would leave and go to his wife's house for the night, but he would return and he and my mother would make up like nothing ever happened. He would beat on her a few days later, and out the window to grandma's house I would go again. This went on and on until one day my mom told me as a punishment, I could not go to my grandmother's house and play or hang out anymore. I was around 12 or 13 at that time. It was devastating to me.

She said, "No matter what went on, I had better not go to my grandmother's house."

During this time, the beatings continued and got worse. I was afraid to disobey her. I would lay there with my hands covering my ears as I listened to her screams as she begged and pleaded for him to stop. Things crashed to the floor. I heard the hard thuds of her body being thrown into the wall. Then the next day, they would be lovey-dovey once again, as if nothing ever happened.

All this time, I grew up right before her eyes and she didn't even see me. She was so caught up in a toxic tumultuous relationship, I became a young woman with no help from my mother. My needs as a new teenager were not assessed. I couldn't go to my grandmother's and I didn't have a voice. *I'm going to kill myself,* I said to myself. I saw it done on TV. I knew how I would do it. My mother doesn't care. *All she cared about was him,* I thought to myself. One night, I decided I would go and take a handful of pills from the medicine cabinet and die. *Here I am 13 years old and I want to die.* Why would that be my thought process at such a tender age?

Nevertheless that was my thought. I took the first handful of pills and I slept and waited for something to happen. Hours went by and I was still alive. *Nothing is happening, why am I not dead?* I remember going back into the cabinet and pouring more into my hand, but this time I mixed them with another bottle that was also in the cabinet. *This should do it,* I said to myself. I took them all and waited.

Our rooms were where we spent most of our time anyways. Not often did she come back there to check on us. The day turned into night. My mom finally called out to us to go to a lady's house that ran a sweet shop inside of her home. I came out of the room and felt hazy, I could barely see or stand up straight. Nevertheless, she never noticed anything different about me. My mother gave us money, told us what she wanted us to buy, then told us to hurry up.

My sister and I ran into the darkness to the sweet shop. My little sister wanted to race with me so we ran faster. The faster I ran, the more I felt like I moved in slow motion. The earth seemingly moved from side to side. We got there and I wasn't able to speak and tell the lady what we wanted to buy. It was like my jaws had locked. My sister spoke up for me. We ran back to my mom's house and I continued to feel the same way. Then it got worse. We opened the door and went inside and I handed my mom the things she wanted. She finally noticed something was off with me and called me into her room. She looked at me and called me by my nickname. I tried to speak. When I did speak, it was in slow motion which was then followed by convulsions. I was having a seizure. I couldn't open my mouth and I couldn't speak.

    The next few weeks would be spent in the hospital with doctors who tried to figure out how to fix what was going on with me. I lied and said I didn't take anything, when I was asked. I was afraid to tell. The seizures continued on and off. I finally had my mom's attention, sad to say. While taking a nap during my stay at the hospital I turned over, opened my eyes and saw my grandmother sitting at my bedside. My grandmother had someone drive her to the hospital so she could be there by my side. She was always there for all of us. She reached out to me and tried to feel where I was in the bed. She laid her hand on my chest as I went in and out of seizures.

    Finally at my grandmother's urging, I told the doctors what pills I had consumed from my mother's medicine cabinet which would help them treat me. This was after weeks of cat scans and threats of a spinal tap which also helped to convince me. After getting my stomach pumped and being treated so that the seizures would stop, I went home and was thrust back into the same house of iniquity. I became invisible once again. The only difference was I decided I didn't want to die anymore. I became numb and acclimated for the moment and tried my best to behave at all times so I could at least see my grandmother. My grandmother's house was my getaway and my solace. Children are a gift and are not asked to be brought into this world. It's our duty as parents to feed their mental stability, to check in with them, and make sure they are okay.

Once a child is born to you, your life is no longer your own. You must give of yourself unselfishly and without failure.

Pay attention to the signs. Be available. Don't get so engrossed in your own world that you lose sight of the special beings God has entrusted you with. If it had not been for my grandmother, I don't know where I would be. Some children are not as lucky to have a place of solace. In speaking today and being alive, I know there's another plan for my life. What could have ended me made me stronger! My life has a purpose. Yours do too.

Your greatest strength shows in the stance you take after you have been tried in the fire repeatedly.....

Y.R. Perry

CHAPTER 9

STOP LETTING HIM BREADCRUMB YOU, SIS!

Often in the dating world, or the game of dating, women can tend to fall victim to the mind manipulation of men. While I am sure some guys go through some of the same things, I'm going to speak from a woman's point of view. Right now, mine. After 10 years of marriage, the first time, and almost seven years the second time, I have now been divorced for 11 years and counting. I have had what I consider a couple of serious relationships, and I also went on a lot of dates. For the life of me, I still don't understand what has shifted, but I know something has. In a world of many beautiful, successful women and men, why are the two so hard to connect? Have you ever met a guy and everything seems great, therefore, you start to date regularly? You talk on the phone and go out, etc. Then all of a sudden, he becomes a little distant with those conversations? He trades those phone conversations for text that consists of WYD, or HRU? You call him and he doesn't answer the phone right then, but calls you back shortly after, maybe 30 minutes to an hour each time. He always has some asinine excuses as to why?

Then your bullshit meter goes off in your gut, and you cut him off. Then all of a sudden, he's calling again, wanting to go on dates and make himself available like he used to. You let him back in and he repeats the same behavior. He's basically breadcrumbing you! Remember the story of Hansel and Gretel where the witch left breadcrumbs in the forest to lure them into her home so she could eat them? It's the same scenario, but slightly different as it pertains to today's dating world. Again I am going to say some men, because I'm speaking from my experience and what I have heard from friends. While I'm sure there are women who do the same, but some men as I was saying, will have you full of hope and promises of something great, then for some reason they will allow things to fall off for a minute.

Maybe he might have lied about his status, he might not be ready to commit or he may not be done playing the field. As soon as you start to catch on, he will begin to drop little breadcrumbs, like I miss you, I want to see you, and blow up your phone because you stopped calling. Women want to believe badly in love and that it still exists. We do this to the point that we will give some men chance after chance after chance, even though the facts are right before eyes. I allowed myself to be breadcrumbed before. I accepted lie after lie, when I knew better, until one day I became sick of it!

I knew my own worth. I wanted more than mere crumbs from a man when I knew I deserved a whole entrée. We are worthy of a man who will keep it one hundred percent with us at all times. We deserve a king who will continuously feed our soul. We don't want a man who is indecisive about us. Self worth for some is sometimes developed over a period of time, after countless episodes of giving of yourself until you grow tired. No one is perfect. Even someone who believes they have the utmost of self-worth may fall victim to this.

Ladies, as the dating world gets harder, whatever you desire, be it to marry again, date seriously, or be happily single, never allow someone to breadcrumb you. Breadcrumbing also comes in many forms and is not always a man of interest that does it. It could be a job that doesn't recognize your full potential to advance, because the powers-that-be want to keep you at a certain level. They give you enough to keep you excited about where you are. This is the same as a friendship that is not equally reciprocated. If you find yourself in a breadcrumbing situation let him, them, or it, go. Sis, you're worth way more than crumbs!

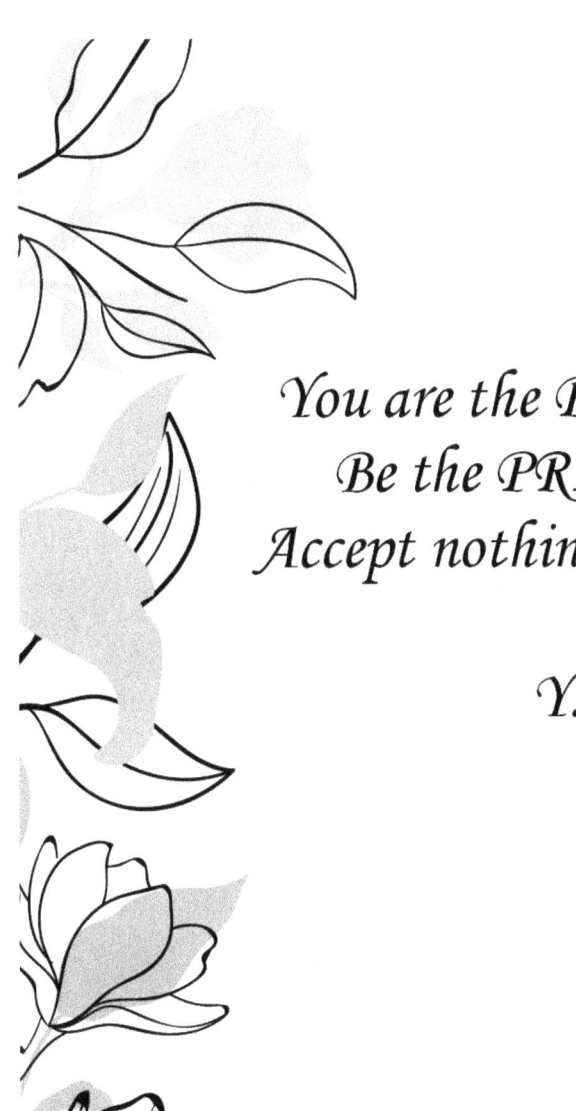

You are the PRIZE!
Be the PRIZE!
Accept nothing less......

Y.R. Perry

CHAPTER 10
BEING AN ENERGY OUTLET

In a house, there are multiple outlets that residents can plug almost anything into. When you want something to work, whether it is a toaster, lamp, or television, etc., the house generally has plenty available sources. Sometimes if they are overused, an outlet can burn out, but that's okay. You can plug the item you want to work into another outlet in the house until you're able to fix it.

We can sometimes become an energy outlet for people. The problem is, we don't have multiple outlets for them to plug into and receive our energy. We only have one outlet and that's our mind. We must be careful who we let plug into us and receive our energy because we can find ourselves depleted and unable to operate or function day to day.

At one point in my life, I had multiple people who I called friends, and some family members I would constantly let plug in to me. I wanted to be that person they could call when needed for assistance, help with something, a shoulder to cry on, or a listening ear. Time after time, I opened myself up and accepted that phone call that went on for hours, or that meet up with a friend at happy hour because someone had a bad day and needed encouragement. I was that friend that if I noticed a social media post from one of my friends and it seemed to call for concern, I reached out to be of encouragement. I cried with and for family members who were stressed and in distress. I tried to be encouraging. This went on until one day I found myself in a place of darkness again. It was one I could not shake and could not understand. Sometimes I laid in bed and cried, not understanding why, unable to move and barely able to shower. Then back in bed I would stay. Nothing had happened to me personally; it seemed like a dark cloud took over my existence. I did the only thing I knew would bring me out. I began to pray. I prayed my way out of it only to continue to be an outlet once again for others and bring myself back to that same state of mind. Once back in that state of mind, I noticed not one phone call came through, there were no invitations to happy hour, no, "Hey girl, I was just calling to check on you." Nothing! I finally figured out the source of why I kept sinking into this dark place.

It was because I continuously allowed people to plug into me and receive so much of my energy, until I burned out. This was much like an energy outlet in a house as I spoke of earlier. The only difference is I had no other outlets in my house, my body. I was depleted and as soon as I repaired myself, I allowed people to plug into me and burn me out again. No one tried to repair me. I had to learn self-healing and separation. Self-healing came through meditation and prayer and the help of God. The separation part was the only thing left. Separation was something I had to undergo in order to be a viable source of energy for myself first, my children, and then others. I became selective of those who would not only plug into me, but also would charge me up if they saw that my energy level was depleted. I separated from friends and also family in an effort to save me so that I would not die spiritually, mentally, emotionally, and maybe even physically.

If you ever find yourself in a dark place, check the energy sources around you. Check your family, friends, and even your spouse or significant other. If they are constantly running on empty and looking for someone to plug into, don't let that source always be you. Unless they are able to pray, self-heal, and be an energy source to you.

People often don't understand the cause of their depression. Most of the time it can be a mental illness, however, it could also be that they have taken on more than they can bear at the moment. They give too much of themselves and try to stay strong for others to the point they simply burn completely out. That burnout can be irreprehensible, and beyond repair to the human mind. Learn ways to self-heal yourself and don't be afraid or feel bad if you are unavailable at times. Take care of yourself first! Give of yourself as much as you can. When you can't, take the time to recharge yourself. Hopefully those who love you, will notice what they are putting you through and be ready with an outlet for you to plug in to, as you have done so for them.

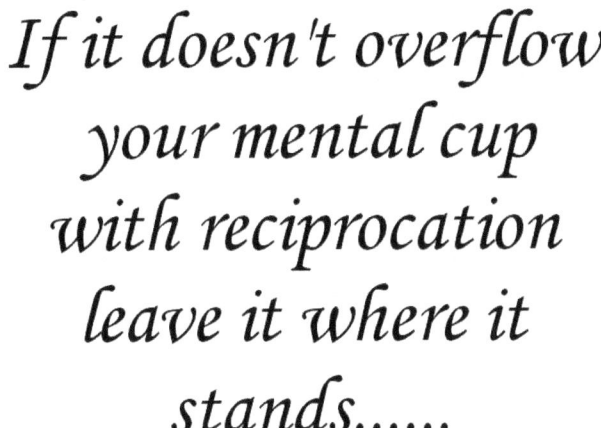

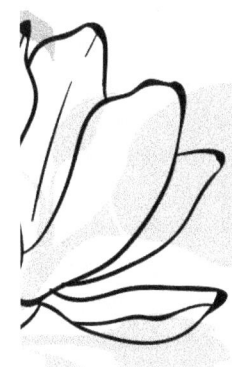

If it doesn't overflow your mental cup with reciprocation leave it where it stands......

Y.R. Perry

CHAPTER 11
EYES FORWARD

Often, there are times when we can't see what's ahead of us because we constantly look at what's behind us. We look at past relationships, past hurt, a goal we tried to achieve but failed at, or whatever it may be. Indeed, there are times we must go backwards in order to go forward, but only in certain cases. Going backwards to go forward means there's something you may need to rectify in order to mentally push forward. You might have to forgive someone in order to be mentally set free. You must remember in order to learn from it so you don't repeat the past.

There's a difference when you constantly look backwards at situations and repeatedly hope for a different result. There were times in my life when God removed me from a situation I prayed and asked him to remove me from, yet I continued to look back and sometimes reach back. Every time I reached back, it set me back. Don't ever ask God to remove something from your life if you plan to reach back and get it. Everything and everyone deserves a second chance, depending on the circumstance, but not a third, fourth, or fifth. Matthew 18:21, 22 says we are to forgive seventy times seven and in doing so, I'm sure God wants us to learn something along the way. In your forgiveness, prayerfully you learn something and make new mistakes to learn from instead of making the same ones.

I strongly believe there are some things that are meant to be blessings or lessons and there's always a blessing within a lesson.

Sometimes it can be obscure because of what the self wants. Have you ever felt like you would be so much further in life, with a project, business venture, or a person, if you would have kept your eyes forward? Once you have prayed for God to remove what you prayed to be removed, keep your eyes forward. There's nothing behind you that you need, if so, it would be in front of you. Think of a time machine. If given the opportunity to go back in time, would you choose to revisit a good time or would you want to revisit a time of misery and distress? Most likely, your answer would be to revisit something amazing and wonderful that touched your heart, or made you a better person. If you are fortunate enough to make it out of a bad situation, and you constantly think back into the past, you're mentally making a choice to pull that lever on the time machine in your mind that may alter your present. I must admit I'm guilty of that and sometimes the road back to happiness is 10 times more difficult to find. Decide to live in happiness, today. Let the past be the past never to be revisited unless it was a time of greatness, things loved, and people who loved you. These are things that will propel you further into a place of peace and eternal happiness.

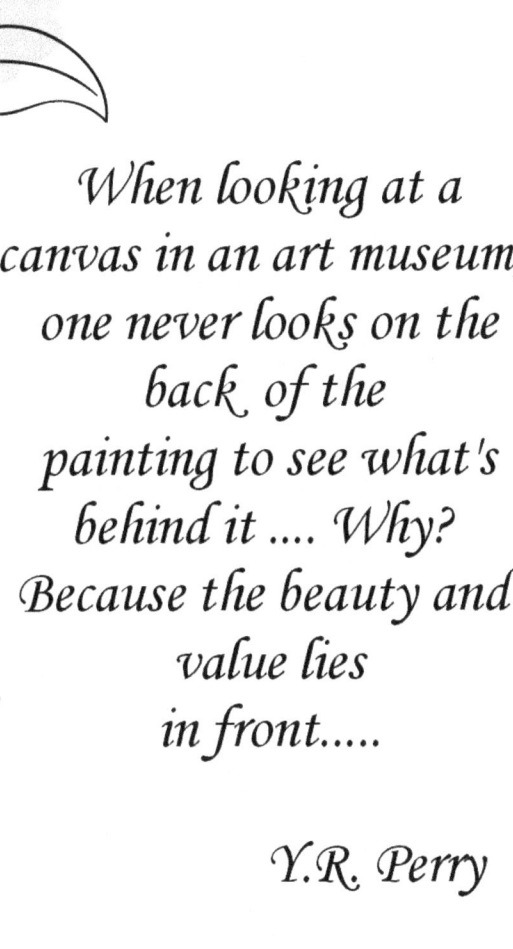

When looking at a canvas in an art museum, one never looks on the back of the painting to see what's behind it .... Why? Because the beauty and value lies in front.....

Y.R. Perry

CHAPTER 12

FRIEND OR F.O.E. (FRIEND OF OPPORTUNITY EXPERT)

If you had to describe what a true friend is, what would your definition be? A dictionary term says, "a friend is a person whom one knows and with whom one has a bond of mutual affection." The key words for this definition are bond and mutual. In calling someone your friend, these two things must be equal and not one-sided. Be careful who you call friend unless friend is a term of endearment that you use to describe everyone. As I raised my two children, I was sure to instill in them the difference between having a friend or an associate. I let them know you cannot call everyone a friend, let alone give any person that title. Being a true friend comes with culpability. That's something everyone is not willing to shoulder. There are also some people who will claim to be your friend when it's convenient. This brings me to my next statement, F.O.E. This is not the usual meaning, but the one I have paraphrased to mean Friend of Opportunity Expert.

I came up with this term because of the mistakes I made in calling someone my friend instead of an associate or acquaintance. In case you don't know, the definition of associate or acquaintance, it is, "a person one knows slightly but who is not a close friend." As much as we would like to believe that everyone has our best interest at heart, some only play the part and are along for the ride and not the journey. A ride is brief, a journey can last a lifetime. Associates ride and when the scenery becomes drab or the destination seems to take too long to get to, they tend to want you to stop and let them out or they begin to complain. They simply exit at some point in your life when you come to a brief stop. A friend, a true friend, will take the journey with you. No matter how long it takes, they are there to gas you up with enthusiasm and encouragement. Even when the journey goes through mountains, over hills, bumps, and potholes, their bond with you is unwavering and unconditional. I have encountered a few F.O.E.s in my lifetime. They are temporary and will show you their hand sooner than later, and often we see it, but we give a benefit of doubt and that's okay. They won't last, because whenever the opportunity you have exposed them to works in their favor or, you begin excelling in areas that they are not excelling in they run out. In dealing with F O.E.s, envy will ultimately rear its ugly head. There is a destination that is designed for you and you only, and possibly a true friend if you're lucky to have one. Know everyone cannot go, nor are they meant to go on your journey. Recognize who is a true friend and who is a F.O.E, a person who befriends someone for the purpose of opportunity only. Find someone who is there for the journey and not just for the ride.

Remember all ducks quack, don't mistake it for rooster call.... You were right the first time you felt it!

Y.R. Perry

CHAPTER 13
ARTICHOKE OR ONION

One night while watching a movie, I heard the question being asked, "Are you an artichoke or an onion?" I found it interesting in how the two were the same, but different. They are definitely not the same in flavor or texture, nor not even in color, but the one main thing they did have in common were layers. Once you start to peel back the layers, you will see only one of them have a heart. In my journey of dealing with people in relationships, I have dealt with several onions and not enough artichokes. In getting to know someone, there are several layers you must go through in order to find out who that person really is. Some of us never take the time to peel back all of the layers of a person or situation.

We are in such a hurry, much like a microwave affect. We want what we want and we would rather have it sooner, than later. We don't know the cost of not taking time to peel back all the layers to get to know the heart of something or someone and that could be to our detriment. Onions are smooth, round, and firm in texture. An artichoke's surface is layered with a crown of pointy fibers. It is not attractive at first glance. Once you start to peel an onion, it begins to release a pungent chemical of fumes that when it comes in contact with the moisture in your eyes, they will begin to burn. How many of us have cut onions non-stop with tears streaming down our face, with a purpose of adding it to something to make it better than it would be without them? My hand is definitely up. With many remedies to lessen the burning sensation of the sufate enzyme, sometimes it still manages to get through and burn your eyes anyway. In my lifetime, I have had many onion type situations in relationships, Situations and circumstances have occurred in my life that constantly keep me in tears. I added myself to the situation thinking that I could make it better, only to end up in tears in the long run.

That was until I learned the difference. I never knew what an artichoke was until I was well into my late twenties to early thirties, the food that is. I soon learned the difference between an artichoke and an onion and how I can equate the two to everyday life and situations. Like an onion, the artichoke has layers you can peel back to get to the center. After peeling layer after layer of an onion with tears flowing and utilizing different remedies to lessen the burn, sometimes it works and sometimes it didn't. Yet, you continue to peel until you get to the center only to discover that is hollow. There's nothing there. A lot of times we make choices in life and we choose things that cause us much pain only to get to the center of it and there's nothing. What was it all for? Were all the tears worth it? Did we make the right choice? What alternative could we have used? We cannot always prevent the trials and tribulations of life for behind every challenge and every tear that has been shed, a lesson was learned. It also builds character and strength. There are certain things we have a choice in. We can continue to choose onions which fail in comparison to the nutritional value of an artichoke.

Even though there are remedies that will lessen the burn to your eyes, you may still shed tears. You say to yourself,

I know there has to be a better way. There's a way that I can have what I want and desire and not go through this pain. Then you're introduced to onion powder or onion flakes. No tears there, right? No layers at all. It is simple and easy. Yet definitely there's no substance. Where's the value? The flavor is not as authentic but it will suffice, right? No layers to go through and still there's no heart. Substitution doesn't necessarily mean better.

Then there's an artichoke. At first glance it is not attractive and the surface seems almost impenetrable. Not knowing that inside lies a heart, soft, complex and meaty, full of texture. It may be a little tough at first to pull back its layers, but it is definitely worth it. The nutritional value supersedes that of the onion. It doesn't make you cry and it's healthy for your heart. All that being said, choose wisely when entering into situations of any kind that appear to be smooth and easy. It's not always rewarding, nor do you have to feel like if tears aren't a part of the process, then it's not a true journey. You can go through all of that and still end up empty at the core. Examine the situations and take the time out to find out what's more beneficial for you in the end. What will add more nutritional value to your mental and emotional state long-term? Now that you know this, when you must deal with an onion, know exactly what you're getting yourself into. Know its value and what you will use it for in your life. Know that it comes in other components that will allow you to get the value without the pain of tears. Recognize and appreciate an artichoke when you see it. It will have layers much like an onion, but once at its core, you will find a heart so tender that you can feast on it and it will sustain you. It has more value than an empty core. The tears shed are only ones of happiness and zero pain. Choose more artichokes.

Sometimes being decieved is a choice, that we all must continue to NOT choose. The truth is in the energy you feel......

Y.R. Perry

CHAPTER 14
WHY BE BEAUTIFUL?

Being in the beauty industry, I have had the pleasure of enhancing or changing something about a woman she didn't quite feel confident about, or that she thought would add more value to her look. Sometimes, she might even want to catch the eye of that certain someone who may have piqued her interest or to ignite the interest of someone whose pique or interest may have plateaued.

I believe 80% of the time women change things about ourselves based upon how we want others to see us first and 20% of the time based on how we want to see ourselves. It should be 100% about us from the beginning and the way we want to see ourselves. Don't get me wrong, there is nothing wrong with looking good for others and the friendly competition and war of looks among women. It is only when you rely on the validation of others in terms of your looks: your hair, makeup, or clothing is when issues arise. In this time of social media and social acceptance, where plastic surgery was once considered a rich white woman's thing, it has now become a favorite pastime for all women. From wigs to hair weaving, breast implants to butt lifts, it has become the rage all over the world with now affordable opportunities. I don't knock anyone who is able to change something that they don't like about themselves to help boost their self-esteem and confidence. However, one must be sure that the inside matches the outside and that you do it for you and not for the masses. I strongly believe that if one never fixes what lives within no matter how appealing the outside is to others, you will still be half the person you can be.

There will be times when you're alone and you must sit with yourself and ask yourself, *does this really make me happy?* Even though you're accepted by others and your popularity may be overflowing, have you accepted yourself first? Only then can your true light shine. Often women change things about themselves hoping to land a man, keep a man, or to get a man to marry them. They go through all of this trouble, only for the man to go out and cheat with a woman who hasn't nearly gone to those levels to get him or keep him. Now you're stuck with the questions, "Why be beautiful?" "Why go to such measures if he's never going to marry me?" "Why get a bigger butt and go through the pain of surgery if he's still going to cheat on me or look at me in a sexual way only?" Those are questions that arise when you must sit with self at the end of the day. Another question we ask is, "Why dress up and put on makeup if women will hate on me and view me as competition instead of an ally?"

When I worked at a prominent, well-known beauty chain, I couldn't count the number of times women would come in and look for foundations and concealers to cover up acne and scars of hyperpigmentation, etc. They only inquired about things that would help them to conceal or hide their flaws, never about what would help them to have less acne. They were only interested in quick gratification. The only problem was that they had to wash it all off and reapply it repeatedly when what they saw in the mirror didn't give that boost of confidence they desired. Much like cosmetic surgery, it's never a one- and-done. It becomes a repeat process to maintain that can be exhausting, expensive, and may even cost you your life.

While working at this chain, I almost became an educator on skin care as I stood in there day after day with wall-to-wall skincare products. It was women of color and for the most part, who never asked about skin care or help in healing what was underneath all the makeup. They could set themselves free without shame and embarrassment of skin conditions, never to use a quick fix again. Until you fix what troubles within and what lies beneath you, you will never be completely free. No matter how you mask it or change it. Gain acceptance from yourself first then others. If you want to change something about yourself do it for Y.O.U.! Don't let the validation of others move you or make you the person you are. When you sit with yourself at the end of the day, you should feel confident and 100% validated because you did it for you. It's only a privilege for anyone else to see it manifest on the exterior. Why be beautiful? The answer is simple. Do it for you, with no expectation from others!

Be your own kind of beautiful, not what the world sees as such, You were born to be your very own Picasso.....

Y.R. Perry

CHAPTER 15
LOUD SILENCE

There was a time in my life where I was forced to sit in silence and be still. Maybe this has happened to you. At a raw point in the world, I lost my job. It was a job that completely shaped my livelihood and the way that I function, to my day-to-day overall well-being. I can't tell you that when I was initially given the news, I wasn't distraught, but in the midst of those feelings, I also felt a sense of peace overcome me. It was unexplainable to say the least. After being walked out of my place of employment, I sat in my car in silence and thought about what had occurred.

Part of me asked, "Why didn't you curse? Why didn't you yell? Why didn't you scream at them? After everything you have done for this company, how dare they?" In spite of it all, I walked out and I remained professional, but in my silent time, alone in my car, I sat in the parking lot of my now former job, and the silence screamed loudly.

"What are you going to do now? What just happened? Why did this just happen to me? This is so unfair!" Even though these questions screamed in my mind, I managed not to shed a tear because there was something in my gut that gave me peace and kept me from acting and overreacting. I started my car. I didn't turn on the music. I left the parking lot and finally took a deep breath while I tried to control my emotions. I drew from that inner peace in my gut as the loud silence began again. The questions in my head brought up the doubt and the pain of what uncertainties lie ahead. That particular day, I had already had a lunch date planned so instead of canceling, I chose to draw from the peace I felt in my gut. I enjoyed my lunch date, with *him* never being the wiser of the traumatic experience I had encountered. I smiled and enjoyed the moment.

Once it was over, on the long ride home, the loud silence began again. I could have easily turned on the music to drown it out. Wrong! When the loud silence in your mind seeks to destroy you, it overpowers and supersedes anything you may try to utilize to drown it out, unless you have that great connection and that connection is one with the Father, the Son, and the Holy Spirit. I carried that connection in the pit of my gut that continued to battle the loud silence in my mind.

When the loud silence would say, "You're going to be homeless now!" the peace in my gut would say, "I have not spoken yet." When the loud silence would say, "You're never going to find a job that pays you what you were making!" the peace in my gut would say, "I have something way better for you!" When the loud silence in my head would say, "You're out of work at your age what are you going to do?" the peace in my gut would say, "It's okay. Soon, people will seek you to work with, and for you!"

You must have a faith factor that will balance you in hard times. If you are not faith-centered, you can easily be destroyed in times like this one. Because of that rested faith in the pit of my gut, I trusted it more than the loud sounds in my head. The loud silence was unable to defeat me. Any time during my alone time, the battle would wage again.

It would be my gut against my mind and my mind would sometimes get the best of me. Then, I would do everything in me to pull from the peace within my gut.

I'm going to be honest with you, at times it wasn't enough. *What do I do now?* I fed my faith, through prayer and positive affirmations for myself. The mind can play dangerous games on you mentally in a time of weakness. The mind is strong! If allowed, it will wear down and take away any faith you have. There's two armies fighting back and forth that can leave you exhausted and depleted. You must make a choice on what you choose to feed, the negativity in your mind or the faith in your gut. I'm a firm believer that faith overpowers all! Continue to feed your faith in times of darkness until that peace you feel in your gut starts to radiate and drown out the loud silence of negativity in your head. That's the loudest silence that no one hears, but it screams in your mind during your quiet times and when you're alone. Feed your faith daily and allow it to take over. It starts with you and you must first believe in you in order for the validation within your soul to drown out the loud silence.

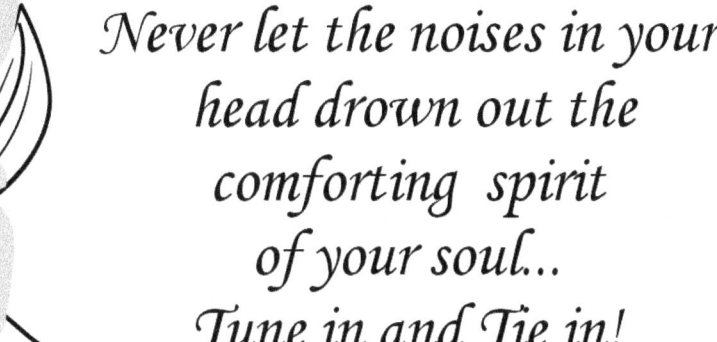

Never let the noises in your head drown out the comforting spirit of your soul...
Tune in and Tie in!

Y.R. Perry

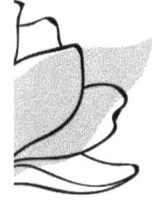

CHAPTER 16

SEEKING APPROVAL FROM THE UNDERQUALIFIED

Have you ever dated someone or made a decision in your life that you were completely happy with? You were all gung-ho and all smiles and extremely confident in your decision? That is, until you shared your great news of that new boyfriend, new job, new business venture, new move, etc., with someone who was underqualified to be an approver of your choices.

People who are underqualified will have you second guessing your whole life. In some instances, the advice they give may be valid. In other cases, it can be envy or an effort to commit sabotage. The misery loves company syndrome, or the lack of motivation and drive on their behalf that you possess, i.e., the crab in the barrel mentality, can definitely be a factor. These people you seek approval from are not qualified to speak on your moves or changes in your life. You say that it doesn't matter what people think, but my answer to you is, if that is so, share less. The less you share with dream stealers and doubt creators, the better. If you choose to share, be sure that the person you share your joy with is 100% qualified to speak on your situation, if approval is what you seek. Sometimes we seek approval without saying it because we give out too much information on what we supposedly have made up in our minds about. We inadvertently listen for a response. Once we do that, we open the door for other things that we were once comfortable with, to be altered. This will also cause us to start the questions in our mind. Then comes the doubt concerning what one was so confident about. When listening to or taking the advice of someone about a situation, person, place, or thing, do a checklist concerning that person. What makes them qualified to cause a shift change in your decision? Those who are deemed qualified may sometimes be able to look deeper into a situation and see things you may not see that are valid. For example, a single person giving a married person advice on marriage, underqualified. A person with no children trying to tell someone with children how to raise children, underqualified. A high school graduate giving a college scholar advice on studies, underqualified. You get the message.

Now switch those examples around and you will see the added value. I'm not saying nothing can come about from the first scenario, but there is a lack of experience of the examples given to be able to effectively speak on such matters. Consider the source of which you seek or allow your decisions to be detoured. Not everyone is qualified to give you advice over your happiness. Moreover, if you are happy and solid in your decision, say less. Only those who seek approval overshare and when you do this, you leave it open for the underqualified to speak on your situation and allow doubt to shake the foundation of what once was solid. When you are firm and solid in your decision, share less and avoid conversations that are important to you with the underqualified because they wouldn't understand. Remember there's a difference between sharing and oversharing.

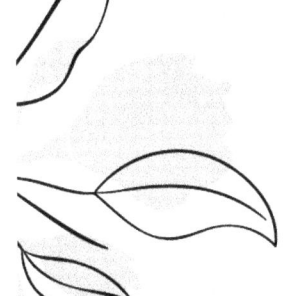

There's no approval that should be sought after more than the one of the almighty God!

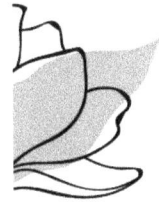

Y.R. Perry

CHAPTER 17

THAT TIME I DECIDED TO LIVE AND NOT DIE

As I spoke about in earlier chapters, the mind is powerful. If you are not mentally strong, a believer in faith, and someone who is able to take a step back and pray, I mean really pray your way through, your mind has the capability of destroying you. When I titled this chapter, "The Time I Decided to Live and not Die," I didn't mean in the physical; I meant in the mental and in spirit. Truth be told, if you allowed those two entities to die, the physical part of you will not be far behind. At the end of the year 2020, the world had changed drastically for me. As I wrote this book, we were in the middle of a pandemic and have been for some time now with no end in sight. Covid-19 has spread all around us. In the U.S., over 541,000 people have died and they are still dying due to this disease.

People have loss their jobs, cars, homes, etc. I thought I was safe, and then it happened to me. The unthinkable. I can't say I didn't see it coming, but never in a million years would I have thought that I would lose my job in the middle of a pandemic! Not with a company I had been with for 20 years.

On November 17, 2020, I was called into my general manager's office and let go of my duties. I was in total and complete shock. Why? How? What type of company would let someone go in the middle of a pandemic that had a 20-

year tenure and a history of increase in profit? In spite of all my questions the fact was I no longer had a job, I no longer had a steady stream of income as I did for years. No one was hiring in the middle of a pandemic!

My time without a job and no source of income, would stretch on during a tumultuous time in the world. I would learn peace that I felt would sustain me and not let me die spiritually or mentally. Over the duration of time I remained unemployed which seemed forever, but turned out to be approximately three and a half months, I fought for unemployment benefits to no avail. I had to allow that peace in my gut to flow upward to my head and give me an overall sense of peace. It was indeed a struggle. Either I allow the confusion and turmoil I felt to flow down and consume me or the peace in my gut to flow upward and release me. How did I get through it you ask? Let me tell you it wasn't an easy task. I had to pray often, pray hard, and pray continuously. There were days I had to talk to myself, as I tried to convince myself to get out of bed. It was really hard, and it happened right before the holidays. I got declined repeatedly for unemployment and my savings got low. What was I to do? I continued to pray. I cried a lot but I also prayed. When I prayed, I initially wasn't praying for a job. At first, I prayed for God to keep me in peace and not allow my head to destroy me. There were lots of sleepless nights where I would lie awake thinking, and asking *what do I do now?*

Visions of me losing my place of residence, having to reside with my children haunted me. I barely left home without forcing myself too. It wasn't often. I didn't get dressed or go out anywhere. I didn't work out. I was lying there mentally dying! Then I decided, "Enough is enough!" I told myself out loud. That was something I got in the habit of doing to keep myself going. I decided to work out one day and then go out to an event later that night. After my workout, I stopped at a dollar store to pick up some items for a toy drive I planned to attend later that evening. As I pulled out of the parking lot of that dollar store, a woman was lying on the grass in a sleeping bag. She slept peacefully in broad daylight without a care in the world. I stared at her for a minute. She was all alone.

I finally pulled out into traffic and I sobbed uncontrollably. I cried for her, but I also cried at the revelation God allowed me to see. The woman slept on the ground with probably everything she owned, and I still had a fully furnished apartment, food in the fridge, and a car to drive. I was killing myself mentally over something that had not happened to me. I cried for what I thought was to come that had not come. This woman was on the ground peacefully asleep in broad daylight without a care in the world. No one bothered her. Then it dawned on me, if God could protect her as she slumbered in broad daylight, if she could lie there and trust that no harm would come to her, why can't I?

After that day, I allowed the power of prayer to fuel the peace in my gut and overpower the chaos and turmoil in my head. Sometimes we have to give ourselves pep talks because others won't understand or can't be there. You must have the will to fight for your life when the only person who is trying to kill you is a reflection looking back at you when you look in the mirror. When you have a true spiritual connection with God, and you're really in tune with your spiritual side, you will get these gentle reminders of where you could be and why your existence on Earth is still required. Covid-19 had not touched me or my children thus far. We are blessed and fortunate. How dare I not live? How dare I not trust? Choose to live and not die!

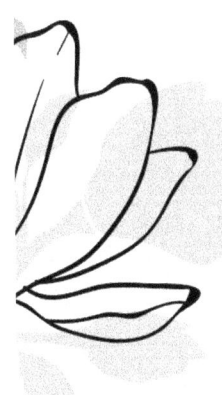

There's someone on the other side that would have loved to have the opportunity you have at this very moment.....
LIFE!
So LIVE!!!

Y.R. Perry

CHAPTER 18

MR. HANDSOME, WELL-TO-DO, AND SIX FOOT TWO?

Every woman wants him, too! We women have in our heads the ideal man we want in our lives. Some of us even make a list and will not deviate from it in the slightest. Sometimes what we see as perfection in the man for us, comes with problems. I'll say it again. With perfection and what we choose as a perfect man for us, sometimes comes problems. In creating these lists or fantasies of what we would prefer in a man, we should first do a self-check of ourselves. Do we have what it takes to lure such a man? What do we bring to the table? Will the scale be balanced? If for some reason you land this perfect man that checks all the boxes on your list and you don't really measure up, are you willing to deal with everything that comes with not checking off all the boxes on his list?

I also had a list. I had the ideal man in my head that I wanted. I knew what he would look like, how he would dress, what his body would look like. I Imaged him coming to scoop me up. He would be rich, tall, and invest in me so I would never have to work again. I felt like I deserved it, after all I had helped build enough men and kissed a few frogs. Why not? I waited, and turned down possibly great men because I had this list. As time goes on and you start to get a little older, you take a look at that list and you ask yourself,

"Do I want to grow old and be alone or do I really want to let someone love me?"

Of course there are certain factors that you can't deviate from when it comes down to deciding what to eliminate from your list and you know the definite deal breakers. Women constantly say there aren't any good men out there, but on the other side of the fence, the men shout the same thing. We've all been hurt to the point we are all afraid. The majority of women say we want consistency, but when we get it, it comes from someone 90% of the time that does not fit the outer exterior of what we had in mind. Without taking the time to get to know what's on the interior, which is the best part, we resort back to our list, and let a beautiful thing pass us by. We don't understand it is the interior where the heart and the soul lies. The interior is far more valuable and greater than the exterior. Physical attributes fade away with age. You must ask yourself, *when that fades, will the heart and soul of that person be enough to sustain you?*

The list that you have, sis, is the same as almost every woman. You wait and so do they, for Mr. Handsome, Well-to-do and Six foot two. By no means am I suggesting that you should settle, but how long are you willing to wait and continue to let the perfect man pass you by? Take the time to get to know someone's heart and soul today that you wouldn't otherwise give thought to, or who may not check off all the boxes on your list. Lessen your list to five must haves and if he checks off three, he's a keeper. Try to eliminate as much of the physical as possible. There's a man out there who is trying to love you and you can't see him because of the idea of what you want, and being selfishly unwilling to look beyond. I guarantee you if you narrow down your list to the five and he checks off three, given the opportunity he will add to your list wonderful things you would have never fathomed or desired. Narrow the list, sis, and let someone love you. I did. Because Mr. Handsome, Well-to-do and Six foot two, just about every woman wants him to, boo!

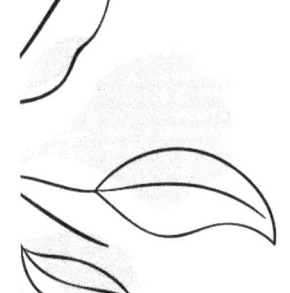

All things rolled into one sometimes leaves nothing up to the imagination.... Absolutely Nothing!

Y.R. Perry

CHAPTER 19

QUIETLY MAKING NOISE

You have probably heard the saying, "Don't announce it until it's done." Often, we get excited and caught up and make an announcement to the world about what's manifested in our lives before the deal is sealed. We make the big mistake of letting everyone know the step by step process of our transitions. That is a big mistake! I'm a firm believer of quietly making moves. People will see your progress without you ever having to say a word. When you announce moves that you make, you open doors for dream stealers and naysayers who will cause you to doubt yourself. I had to learn the hard way. I feel I could have been much further in life had I not allow certain people to know my next moves. People are sometimes like a praying mantis, which is a voracious predator type insect. In short, a praying mantis type person is one who will pray or prey upon every idea you bring forth and devour them for themselves or turn you against your own thoughts and create doubts in your mind. This will slow your progression.

When you sit in silence, your best ideas and thoughts come about. This is where there are no distractions, only silence. The only person you need to hear from during this time is the Holy Spirit. You get your best answers in your quiet time and meditation time. Any doubt that you may have will be revealed and overcome. God provides us with everything we need to be great in this world. It's up to us, as to how we bring those gifts to life. Stop relying on other's opinions of your aspirations and dreams. We have all been given gifts that are left up to us to discover, believe in, and bring forth light to.

Sometimes, when we share, we allow what was once a raging fire of ideas to be smoldered by a naysayer or dream snatcher, who possibly lack the creativity and the willpower you possess. They don't have the wherewithal that it takes to make it happen for themselves. Therefore you become their prey. The only voice you need to hear from is the voice within you and the spirit that surrounds you. Be still, listen, and continue to quietly make noise until it becomes a violent roar created by you and only you.

In your winning season turn up the volume until the world goes silent to listen!

Y.R. Perry

CHAPTER 20

HEY, DARK AND LOVELY

Those are words that would change the way I viewed myself and give me confidence that would last a lifetime. I grew up in the 1980s as a little girl with dark skin and it was not easy. I was picked on and called many names like, Blackie, Tar-Baby, burnt toast, soot black, and the list goes on and on.

I came from a family that didn't have much. At times when my mother often didn't make the right monetary decisions, it meant we went without. That meant not having the best of clothing and sometimes even food. I could sometimes hide not having food, but the fact that you had on hand-me-down clothes that were out of style, on top of being a skin shade that was not desirable to even my own kind, hit hard as a young woman.

When I lived in Oakland, California, it was a blessing and a curse for me. It was a curse because it was a place my grandmother begged my mother not to move to. It wasn't because it was the worst place to possibly ever move to, but because she would not be there to help us. If my mom didn't have it, she wouldn't be able to be there to pick up the slack, be that it was food, clothing, or a place to run to when my sister's father went on one of his abusive tirades. I will never forget the trembling in her voice and the tears in her eyes when she begged my mother, "Please don't take those kids that far away. I won't be able to help you."

Nevertheless, she took us anyway. Sure enough there were times we experienced hunger, went without lights or water and faced eviction. That would be the life I would grow accustomed to. I was new in the area, new to high school, and a dark-skinned freshman carrying way more than I should on my shoulders due to my home life. I did the best I could to fit in and keep my head up. I joined ROTC and tried out for cheerleading. That would be my only solace of mental escape. I dreaded the thought of going home and I wished I could go to my grandmother's house as I did before.

That wasn't going to happen. I had to keep pushing. I was determined not to be a victim of my circumstances. I was always good at doing hair so my hair stayed on point and I made those hand-me-downs look as stylish as I possibly could. Each day, I would walk to school and halfway there, I would stop at a friend's house, meet up with her, and we will continue on to school together. We would do the same thing on the way home.

One sunny day, my friend went her way and I continued on to mine, dreading it the whole way because I never knew what the rest of the day or night would bring. Will there be food? Would we have lights? Will there be water to bathe? Will this be a night that he decides to beat my mom? If I could have lived at school, I probably would have. It was the only time I felt free. En route to my house, dark-skinned me did the best I could with what I had.

I heard a voice say, "Hey, Dark and Lovely."

I turned to see where those words came from and there was this nice looking man sitting outside of his home. He smiled at me, and he repeated it once again. "Hey, Dark and Lovely."

I spoke back and said, "Hi," in a shy manner and then continued on my way home. I thought all the way home, *someone thinks my dark skin is lovely.* This particular day, no matter what went on at home, those four words carried me through. All of the self-doubt and not feeling pretty because of my complexion and not having the newest fashions, the mere fact that this handsome guy thought my dark skin was lovely, made my entire day.

From that time forward, each day I would walk home from school after my friend and I parted ways and like clockwork he sat outside his home and he would see me and would say it again, "Hey, Dark and Lovely."

I would reply, "Hi."

One would probably think this man was trying to lure me in and be fresh with me, but he never tried. He would only speak to me daily on my way home. It got to the point where I couldn't wait to pass his house to hear him say those words. It made me feel great about myself. It made me want to strive harder with things I did have and hold my head up because I was dark and lovely! It didn't matter what the masses said. After some time, the man seemingly disappeared. I don't know, maybe he moved away. I only know I didn't see him anymore.

He didn't know at that time he instilled confidence into a girl who had none. He made me feel beautiful. He gave me a little slice of heaven to think about while living in a home full of chaos. If you can imagine being out in the hot sun and everyone around you sweating from the intensity of the heat, but you are the only one smiling and not sweating at all, because you have an industrial fan blowing only on you. That's how those words made me feel each day When I made it home to a house of hell, it was the one thing that kept me cool in spite of anything that went on. I wish I knew who he was or where he was today, I would thank him because he changed part of my life immensely. Those words remained my happy thoughts. *I may not have the best clothes but I am dark and lovely! I might not live in the best house under the best circumstances, but I am dark and lovely!*

The man didn't know he shaped my thought process around the color of my skin. Those kind words gave me the boost of confidence that I needed in a world that I doubted I would ever be beautiful enough to be recognized in. Compliment someone today. You never know the doubts that lie beneath what appears to be a most beautiful face. Words can sometimes shape the person we are destined to become. A kind soul instilled confidence in me without knowing my story. I will forever see myself as dark and lovely no matter who says differently!

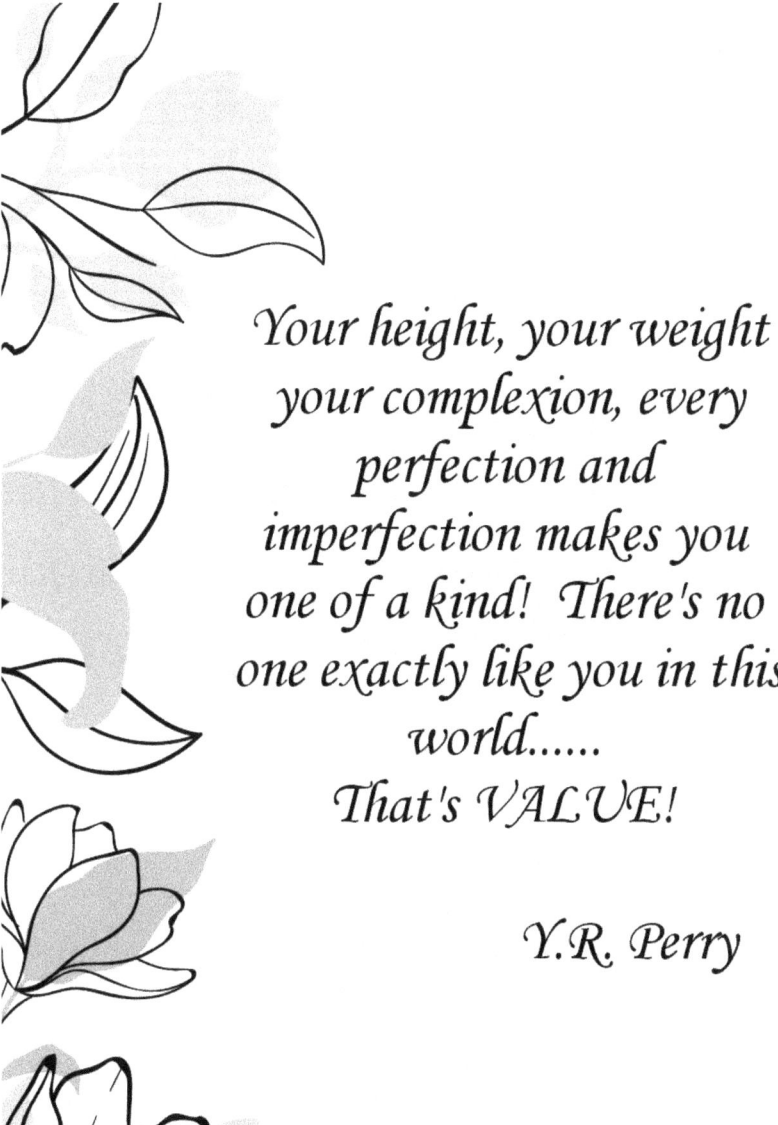

*Your height, your weight your complexion, every perfection and imperfection makes you one of a kind! There's no one exactly like you in this world......
That's VALUE!*

Y.R. Perry

CHAPTER 21
UNPACKING PAIN

Mental pain is a heavy burden to bear and can have many layers to go through before healing can begin. Some people utilize therapists and others seek the spiritual side, or a combination of both. More often than not, therapy is sought in many aspects, leaves no mental resolve. Not resolving mental pain in my opinion can lead to a lifetime of depression, self-loathing, self destruction, bad choices, and even death. Today's world has made it easier to identify these things.

When I grew up, there wasn't such a thing as therapy as far as I know, in the black community. You would either go to church and pray or keep your problems to yourself. Or you would get labeled as crazy, and be given what my grandmother would call a crazy check. No one ever talked about what was going on and the demons they battled. Many things were hidden and accepted like child molestation and spousal abuse. Not having a form of mental release can take a serious toll on a person. A lot of my elders and family members went to their grave labeled crazy and mentally unsound and that was that. But why? They never shared what plagued them and no one ever bothered to ask.

I grew up and became a young woman. No one asked me either. I was fortunate enough to have an aunt who introduced me to church as a little girl and another who followed up where she left off. When I became a young woman with children, it would be the main thing I would rely on in my time of mental struggle. When I felt like I couldn't talk to anyone or no one bothered to ask, "Are you okay?" I took up journaling as a way to unpack my thoughts. It was such a relief! Things would come to my mind that I didn't understand. I wanted to share my feelings and I didn't know how. When I was afraid, or even when I wanted to cry but didn't want anyone to see, I put my words on paper. It was my therapy along with my faith in God and prayers. I couldn't afford a psychologist so this was my best alternative and it would turn out to be the best decision I could have made.

Once I became a mother, I knew it was no longer about me. I knew I would never be able to choose me first again. They would have to be first. By choosing them though, in a way, I guess you could say I had to choose me first. I had to choose to be mentally sound, in order for me to instill values and character into them. I had to choose to remain spiritually connected to share with them that when they felt lost, they should fall on their knees, seek faith, and pray. I had to choose physically to stay strong and healthy that as long as there was breath in my body, I could be the one they could turn to whenever they needed someone to talk to. Also, when I saw the things they may have been unable to speak about, I could ask them, "Are you okay?" Some mental things are beyond our limits and out of our control. If we see someone struggling, stop them and ask, "Hey, are you okay?" Sometimes all you have to do is lend a listening ear to someone. You have no idea the wonders it would do.

One day, I spent over 30 minutes in a parking lot talking to an older lady about her cats. What started as a "hello" and her admiring the way I looked that day, turned into a 30-minute conversation. About five minutes in, I could tell she was lonely and she lived alone. I continue to oblige her with conversation because she seemed elated to talk to someone. Although the time we took would make me late for work, it was worth it to see the joy on her face of being able to share her story with someone. She also talked about her son who made her move in with him, because he felt she wasn't capable of living on her own anymore since her husband passed away.

"What a blessing to have that option. Most people don't," I told her.

I mentioned this story to say everyone is not crazy; they just haven't found an outlet to unpack their pain. They hold on to it, or in some cases they are afraid to share it. Oblige someone in a conversation today that may feel the need to talk, even if it takes a little away from your time.

If you see someone that may be struggling, ask, "Are you okay?"

They may not share anything with you, but the mere fact that you asked them let them know you noticed them and you cared enough.

I saw that older woman again at a different location. What a coincidence. She recognized me and thanked me for talking to her and shared with me her transition into her son's home. Wouldn't you know we ended up in another 30-minute conversation? LOL. And if I ever see her again, I would do it again because it's only a little piece of me that I could share with someone who may need it. It didn't cost me anything but time. I am blessed, fortunate, and most certainly grateful to have time given to me and be able to extend to someone who needs it.

Detox your life of all things unfit that weigh you down. Anything that doesn't help your boat stay afloat must be tossed over board.....
Don't SIT and SINK!

Y. R. Perry

CHAPTER 22

AM I GOOD ENOUGH?

The answer is ABSO-FUKN-LUTELY! We all have questioned ourselves at some point in our lives, wondering if we were good enough. Be it good enough to get a job we desire, good enough to raise successful children, or even good enough to attract a great man. As women, we do things to ourselves to make us feel good about ourselves. We usually do not want to go unnoticed by others. This is especially true when it comes down to attracting the opposite sex. After my last divorce, being on the dating scene was the worst thing ever. Trying to figure out what men like physically; hair long, hair short, hair weave, no hair weave, long nails, short nails, natural or relaxed hair, thick, thin, or BBW. I mean the list goes on and on. Some would even say, "I'm just going to be me, and he's going to have to love me for who I am and how I am."

It all sounds good until you find yourself alone wondering why you are alone and asking yourself, "Why am I not good enough?" Only the real with admit it and only the real will relate. No matter how strong I was or how independent I became, I still desired the companionship of a significant other. Not just anyone, but someone designed especially for me. Although I have settled it, two, or maybe three or four times, (but who's counting?) after finding myself alone, mid-forties vastly approaching, I decided to do a self-assessment. It was time to do a bait change. After all this time, I hadn't attracted Mr. Right for me yet, so I figured it was time to upgrade some things about myself. Not that I wasn't perfect the way I was, however men are visual creatures, their likes and dislikes change like the weather in Houston no matter what was predicted. So just like those impromptu weather changes, we women must stay prepared. When I say bait change, I'm speaking in terms of fishing but in this case, not fishing for the scaly ones that swim in oceans, lakes or ponds, but the two legged ones that walk on land.

My father was an avid fisherman and one thing I learned from him is that in order to get the big fish you must use the best bait. In doing a self-assessment, I felt in order to attract a different type of man, I needed to put some new bait on the hook. That usually includes, new hairdo, clothing style change, different makeup, a little weight loss, or a little weight gain. You do these things, and like a fisherman, you put your bait out then you sit and wait to see what bites. Sometimes it takes a little while and you must wait a little longer. Days may go by and nothing happens, then all of a sudden you get a little tug on your line. It's strong, therefore you pull on that line with all your might, trying to reel it in. It feels like a big one, like it's the one! It may be worth the trophy you think. Only to spend all that time tugging and pulling to reel in a garfish when you had hoped for a blue marlin.

What do you do? You throw it back. Do a bait switch and repeat the process. You repeat the process many times until you ask yourself, *what's wrong with me? Should I lower my expectations and standards?* The answer is no. Should you change up a little bit at time to attract something you may seek? Of course. But most definitely not to the point of losing yourself. A little change is always good even if it's only for you. At one point in my life, I found myself in a bit of a bait switch marathon that went on for some time.

Every time one of my male friends would tell me, "Guys I know like this type of woman, who wears her hair like that, or weighs this amount, or dresses like this," so on and so forth, I would change.

I became exhausted with all of it and said, "You know what? I'm going to do me."

I may get lonely sometimes, but I refuse to settle. Then one day without effort that blue marlin jumped right out of the water and landed in my lap. I didn't have to fish for it. The problem was I kept fishing in that same lake hoping that my trophy fish would one day get caught on my line, but it wasn't there. It wasn't until I changed my direction, my thought process, and allowed the bait switch to be about me, then he came along. He was always there. He watched every switch and admired them all. Redirect your mindset, make the change about you and what you seek. I am enough! And so are you. What you desire will find you, or maybe it has been there all along.

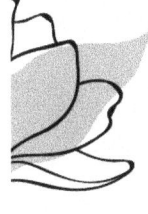

*Show people who you are!
Never question your value.
Question those that don't
see the value in YOU! Then politely
escort them from your
presence IMMEDIATELY!*

Y.R. Perry

CHAPTER 23
I SURRENDER

The word "surrender" means to cease resistance, or submit. When you have no choice in your life but to always be in control, or when you have relinquished control to someone you felt you could trust, only to have them run you off a ledge, surrendering can be hard in all aspects to say the least. Whether it's surrendering to the ways of God, surrendering at your job to make work-life balance easier for you, or surrendering to letting someone into your life after you have been hurt countless times can be hard. Being forced to be in control because you can't trust anyone or anything is a horrible place to be. Most of the time people we consider control freaks have developed this trait because, somewhere in their life they surrendered and someone or something made them regret it. So the mindset of "I will never allow this to happen to me again kicks in." Heaven forbid if they have surrendered more than once or twice. That wall gets higher and higher and the need to be in control gets stronger and stronger.

This was me. My past hurts and disappointments put me in this mindset. Not realizing that when you feel the need to be in control all the time you're resistant to learn or be open to new things, which can hinder your development. You don't believe or trust anything right off hand that anyone says or does. You have to fact-check it. You're reluctant to trust or delegate things, out of fear that it won't be done correctly, and if you do, you have to go back and check to be sure that it is done properly and as delegated. Now don't get me wrong sometimes it's needed, but if it's a constant way of life for anyone it can become a cold, lonely, and miserable existence.

I became, I would say, somewhat of a control freak due to past transgressions with people I trusted with my time, and my heart. Also due to people being put in positions to nurture and educate me but didn't have a clue how to do so. They were just given a position. So once I was in the same position, I vowed always to know what I needed to know first and to be able to educate and nurture anyone beneath me. You might say, well that's great, and yes it was to a certain degree, but it made me less open to change. Why? Because I didn't trust anyone but myself. It also kept me somewhat stagnant in my position as a woman who wanted to find love again and as an employee who wanted to excel from my current position. Holding on to past hurt or mistrust of others can prevent you from receiving the very thing you continually pray for and constantly do not receive. Even though you ask, you are not fully able to receive because you are afraid of losing control.

Once I became a manager of a company, I vowed that I could never work as a regular employee again, unless I was in control. Past jobs failed me, because management put above me, failed to educate me on my position, henceforth setting me up for possible failure. So I started to educate myself more on any position I ever stood in at a workplace, and in doing so, it became my way, and nothing else outside of that made sense to me. The same went for relationships. Once I had been hurt, trusting my heart first and not listening to my gut, like I should have from the beginning and it failed, the need for control grew. This need was taking over my life! It was my way or the highway. After coming to terms with the fact that it was not just them, it was me, I began to seek out relationship advice. Be it from TV shows, Scriptures from church, quotes, etc., I took bits and pieces from it all and collaborated my way of how my next relationship should go. I was not going to waver from it, after all, this advice that I gathered came from quotes, church, and failed marriages. I thought I was on the right track. What I didn't include, is that each situation is different and what works for some doesn't work for all and what didn't work for some does not mean it will not work for me.

Being in control became a miserable existence for me and it was not because I truly wanted to be in control anymore, but after so much time had passed I was afraid to relinquish the reins and trust again. Part of me wanted to, but I just didn't know how to anymore. I knew I had to surrender. How will you ever know if that job you dream of, or if that person is right for you if you don't truly surrender? I'm not saying surrender your whole self but be open to learn other ways other than yours. Surrender slowly of course. The person who you want and really wants you will show you why you are worth it and it won't be with things that money can buy but you will definitely know it. Also, the job you feel you want, but need to be in charge in order to feel validation, be open to play the student. Just surrender.

You must first be open to learning new things. The world is changing rapidly and we have no choice if we are fortunate enough to open our eyes each morning, to also change with it. Don't let hurt stop you from receiving Divine Destiny because you're not willing to trust again. Be open to change, and resistant to your own ways. Trust me I understand that it's hard but, know this the power of growth ceases when you are not willing to surrender. You are not always right no matter how many degrees you have, no matter how many boards you may sit on, no matter how many rooms you are privileged to be in with some of the highest of the upper echelon. There's always more. More to learn in the world and more to learn about love and loving yourself. In return this will help you love others. Unarm yourself of control and surrender, watch how life unfolds. Heal yourself first. Surrender from the heart, trust and grow. It's so much more to know.

Give yourself permission to grow by letting go!

Y.R. Perry

CHAPTER 24

THE COMING OF ME

As I healed myself, and became whole, mind, body and spirit, I felt my value. It radiated from the inside out. I got more in touch with my spiritual side, the side that housed my spiritual energy. I became more cognizant of who was for me and who wasn't.

No longer did I allow what I thought I wanted to overrule my thoughts without first weighing everything out. I used to get so excited about the thought of something before it had manifested itself in the physical. I had not thought it out clearly, before sharing it with everyone. I never understood that some people have the ability to make your dreams their reality before you can make it yours. I had to learn that the hard way.

Soon I began to keep my thoughts, dreams, and passions to myself. I let them manifest in my mind before I manifested them in the physical and was definitely careful of getting so excited, that I shared it with the wrong person or persons. A wise person one told me, even though you might have made a mistake and shared your ideas with someone who took it and made it their own, know that they will never be able to duplicate them verbatim unless you give them the blueprint.

Dealing with life and making out okay and also maturing, put me in touch with my spiritual energy. Some of my best moments and outcomes came about when I sat still and just listened. Not to someone but to your spiritual self. Your spiritual energy will steer you in the right direction and it will also set up alarms within you when something is not right or right for you. When you clear your mind, allow yourself to heal and become whole, another world opens up. That world will be one of amazing ideas and prosperity, but it's up to you to make use of it. Many things always come to my mind in the wee hours of the morning. My mind would begin to race and I couldn't sleep. I started keeping a notepad in my bed to write down everything that came to mind that was of value.

Ideas vividly showed up in my mind as things propelled me further. Then I began the process of manifestation without speaking a word to anyone, just keeping it to myself. There were things I wanted to shout about and tell everyone, but my dreams were not for everybody's ears, nor should yours be. Sometimes your dreams are not for your best friends or even your family to know. You will be surprised who silently competes against you. Continue to move in silence and always stay prepared for the naysayers, copycats, and dream snatchers. Everyone does not have a creative mindset. That's why investors exist. They look for the perfect idea from a creative mind to invest in. Be sure to put a price on your creative mind. Don't give away your dreams for free.

It's time to step into your light! The stage awaits you and there is an audience is shouting your name!

Y.R. Perry

CHAPTER 25

THE STRAW THAT COULD HAVE BROKE ME BUILT ME

You may be familiar with the phrase, "That was the straw that broke the camel's back." Some things that come against you to break you, were also designed to build you. It depends on your will and refusal to be broken. I actually think that's the way God intended for it to be. He tests your will as well as your faith and belief. Often we are broken down to the point we can't fathom the idea of ever being whole again. There are no sources around, to pull strength from, no one to pour into you. You ask, "Why me?" I say, why not you? I'm here to tell you that there is purpose in your pain. It's said that God gives His toughest battles to His strongest. Your will has to be stronger than your woes. As I write this, I am embarking on the age of 48 years old, and in my 48 years of living on this earth, I have run across many wolves. Being broken again is not in my design anymore. It is my will to stay healed and never dwell in brokenness again.

As of this date, I have not spoken to my mother in a year-and-a-half now. That's by her choice, not mine. I have tried repeatedly of course, and it has been to no avail. Just when I thought I had gone through enough and was making my way out of things, now this. "Why Lord?" I asked. "What could I have done to the woman who gave me life that would make her desert me yet again?" All I ever wanted was a mother who would be there, someone I could share things with, get great advice from, and have a shoulder to cry on. I wanted a mother who would say, "Everything will be okay," when I went through my job loss, but much like before, she wasn't there. What now? People would always tell me, "Keep reaching out. She's your mother. You only get one mother." So I did, again it was of no avail. The more I tried, the more the foundation I built for myself to stand on began to crumble again. I would tell myself, *it's okay, I'm over it,* but inside I was crying and in my alone time I would cry outwardly. Then something would say, *she's lost right now.* I would wonder, *is she praying for me like I pray for her? Does she realize even though I only get one mother, there's only one me?* I had a choice to make. I could let this break me and set me back to a place I worked hard to come out of or I could let it build me.

I've heard the phrase, "There's nothing like a mother's love." It's unfortunate for me that I may never know what that feels like, but I can tell you this, my children will know without a shadow of a doubt. I began to feel that if I can survive in this world without the love of my mother, there's nothing I can't make it through. I love my mother and I will to the day I no longer exist on this earth. I don't know the demons she battles so I will continue to pray until God leads her back. I know in her own way, she loves me too, but I choose not to reside in that brokenness anymore. Being broken and choosing to stay broken is a choice. Are you willing to say, "I refuse to stay broken?" If the one thing that should have broken me didn't, it's all oky and universe from here on out.

Sometimes, God will remove the person who can keep you in a place of brokenness, and you will be surprised who that person may be. I believe it's true that God gives the biggest challenges to the strongest. Diamonds are formed from pressure and heat and are also one of the strongest materials on earth.

Today, I stand through intense fires of life, extreme pressures of hurt, pain, sorrow, and disappointment. I stand stronger than ever and all the things that may have been designed to break me, built me. Here I stand, a diamond! My prayer is that whoever reads this book knows they are worthy. Everything you're going through in this life is aligned with your diamond status. Your trials are for sharing, and your testimony needs to be heard by someone's ears. Somewhere, someone feels like they can't make it through. If you're reading this at the moment and that someone is you, all I have to say is, "Hey, there, Diamond. I rebuke the spirit of brokenness in your life, right now in Jesus' name, amen!"

You have survived the worst of times and the best of times... Don't allow the worst to break you because the best will be a grand reward........ Keep holding!

Y. R. Perry

For all of my *Tumultuous* and *Tumuluous Too* readers: Everyone wants to know who picked me up from jail? Man came to pick me up from jail that day, but it was God who came to my rescue as you see He's done many times before.

Continue to pray and stay encouraged!

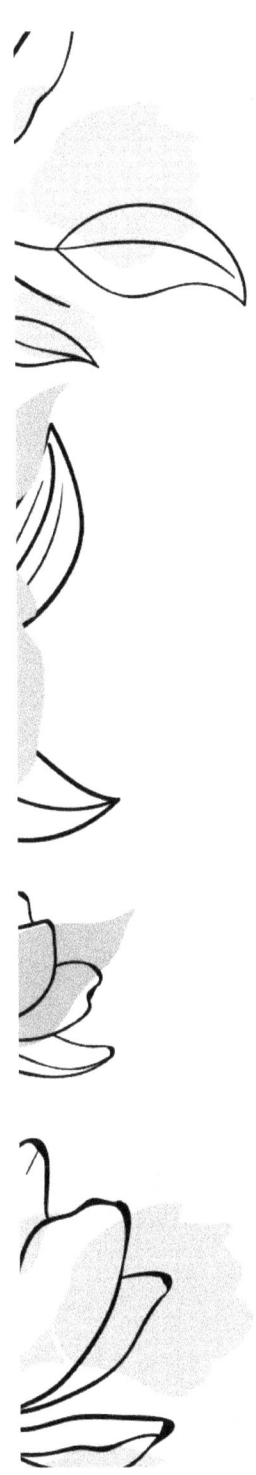

To contact Y.R. Perry, write:

author_yr.perry@yahoo.com

or follow her at:

author_y.r.perry (Instagram)

www.ingramcontent.com/pod-product-compliance
Lightning Source LLC
Chambersburg PA
CBHW050641160426
43194CB00010B/1761